EVOLUTION OF A BUTTERFLY'S TRUTH
Copyright © 2019 by La'Shawn Janell

All rights reserved. No part of this book may be reproduced or transmitted in any form or by any means without written permission from
the Author or Publisher.

Published by:
Ware Resources and Publishing
www.wareresources.com

1-888-469-4850 Ext. 2

ISBN 978-0-9844685-7-7
L.C.C.N: 2019904217

Printed in USA by Ware Resources and Publishing

Autograph Page

_____

_____

_____

_____

Table of Contents

- Introduction 8

Book 1: I am Divine.

- My Plea to God…… ....…...….11
- Restore my Strength….…............................….13
- Lean on Him….….....……..............................14
- I Need You Now ……………………………….15
- My Cleansing ………...…...................………16
- The Wrong Train …………………………..….18
- Runaway Slave …………………………….…..21

Book 2: I am Empowered.

- Ode to my Sistren……………….…….…….…26
- At the Corner of Wisdom and Wonder……………..28
- Which Black/What Black……………………....29
- Code-Switch This…………………………….....32
- A Scoff to a Poor Offer………...……………….34
- Roses……………………………………………35
- The Sun Setting on Hope……………………….37

Book 3: I am Enlightened.

- The Cost of Sight……………………………….42
- For What do we Zoom………………….…..……….45
- Choking on Commercialism……………………….47
- Sorrowful Palm Readings……………………...49
- Social Shackles…………………………………50
- Coming Now, Nonsense……………………….52
- One Step/One Voice………………………...….54

Book 4: I am Loving.

- Manifesting Destiny……………………...…….58

- ❖ Letter to my Future Husband………………......…...63
- ❖ Daybreak after Darkness……………….....……. ..66
- ❖ Hesitantly Speaking………………………......………..68
- ❖ The Throb of Yearning……………...……………71
- ❖ Is it Okay? …………………………………………..72
- ❖ He is My…………………………..........……………76
- ❖ A Pause in Time.…...…………………….....………79
- ❖ Nudity of the Soul. ….…………………….……...…81
- ❖ Liberated Harmony………....…………………..……82

Book 5: I am Sensual.

- ❖ Dimly-Lit Caresses.…....…………………………...86
- ❖ The Intensity of Fusion.…...……………………….88
- ❖ The Great Orators……………………..….……….90
- ❖ Love Song……………………………………...…..92
- ❖ Flirting with Flashbacks………………………..….94
- ❖ Morning Musings…………….....………………….95

Book 6: I am Evolving.

- ❖ Opaque Reflections of Clarity………....……………...98
- ❖ Inverse Reality…………………………....…………99
- ❖ The Price of Competence…………….....…………100
- ❖ Atmospheric Shifts……….....……...………………101
- ❖ Homage to Stevie………………………….………102
- ❖ Familial Patterns……………………………...……103
- ❖ Pursuing Foreverland……………….....……..……105
- ❖ Pressure-filled Intentions………………....………106
- ❖ Plight of a Healer….……………………….………108
- ❖ Simple Rules…………………….....………………110
- ❖ Who Heals the Healer…………….....……………111
- ❖ Will You Be There ……………….....…………..…112
- ❖ Glowing Innocence……………….....………….…114

Book 7: I am Resilient.

- ❖ Eagerly Anticipating…………………...……………117
- ❖ Fleeting Recollections…………………......………118
- ❖ I Needed You………………………....……………122

- ❖ A Half-Full/Half-Empty Greeting………...……………..125
- ❖ Cocoon……….…...126
- ❖ Dieu M'Envoie des Fleurs………....….................…………132
- ❖ Dreams Deferred by the Clock…....………………….…...134
- ❖ As I Escape to Slumber…....…….……………………….....136
- ❖ Letter to My Angel…...…………………………………..138

Introduction

I want to say something...
Something that moves you
Improves your way of thinking
Expands your mind far beyond
The boxes carved into your existence.
I want you to get out of those
And create your space to be whomever you are
When no one is watching.

I want to say something
Bend language in a way you've never heard before
Stretch metaphors beyond your imagination
Break the monotony of ordinary prose
Snap the continuum of regular
I want you to hear *me*
I want to speak to your soul, Friend
Familiarize yourself with the "you" you won't show to outsiders
I want to pull that out of you when I speak...

I hope my words reach you
Teach you a few things you didn't know
See, many think they have me figured out
By labels
By appearance
By highlights
But my writing, greater than any assumption
Is a window into my truth.

I hope when you look in
That you see all of me
Not just what looks good
But the ugly scars I've covered up from falling

My calling, I believe
Is for you to relate
For you to take in my reality
And realize we've all been "here"
That you're not alone
That the human experience is bound together by Love
Pain
And Suffering.
I'm not buffering you from my darkness
You're in
The only sin is if you don't lean *in*
And ask a question or two
I'm opening the door for you...
So, I'll let you drive where we go
Just know
I welcome your dialogue
No one needs to be left in a fog of wondering
Nor questioning
This is a beckoning for us
To get to know each other better
Hello.

Book 1: I am Divine.

My Plea to God

Lord, please accept my tears as my acceptance of You into my heart.
Washing Your grace and glory over me,
I feel weak with the evil You are ripping out of me with every sob
I feel You deep within my soul, mending broken seams
It seems I've been distant, not away just not as close as I should be to You.
So, these tears are an apology -
A decree that I thank you for welcoming me back, Lord.
I've stored up so many shortcomings and masked them with foundation and blush,
But the foundation is You!

You brought forth these tears -
So that my true self is revealed.
Humbled and bowed down before You,
Swaying me with melodies of praise and worship
Praying the seeds You've bestowed upon me are sewn in Your Image
Your light.
I wish my salt to sprinkle upon those who need me,
And with Your help, I will walk Your path.

Lord, the heaves overtaking my small frame are a reminder that
Things are so much bigger than me.
Hence, I receive what is happening to me physically is only the
Start of what You will be to me in this Light
Darkness is defined as merely the absence of light
So please shine Your beam over the corners-
That no one else dare touch
Illuminate the dank, foul pieces of me that have spoiled
Heal me.

Restore me.
I implore thee, please keep showing me the way

I walked into your house today feeling lost yet guided
And was provided such warmth and welcoming that I knew Your Hand held mine as I took steps in.
You carried me and said
"Listen my child, I love you."
"Let my earthly disciples speak my words"
"Hear Me."
And with that, streams poured out…
Not of sadness
But a release that finally I am where You want me
A release that halted resistance.

I felt no shame as Your beams bursted out within me -
Displayed in life's water.
I welcome it.
Please continue to work on me, Lord
And however I show my gratitude
I know You will receive it with open arms
Just as your vessels did with me today
Thank you.

Restore my Strength

Break these chains!
Snap me out of being a slave to irrational thoughts and behaviors.
Be my savior with Your Light and Way.
Walk with me on the road You've written for me.
Show me the bumps so I don't get bruised or misused,
Unless there's a lesson behind You allowing the pain.

Carry me when my legs get weak.
Be my footprints I can follow so this world doesn't swallow me whole.
Continue to be my shore,
Reminding me this puddle of trouble ain't nothing but something to get over.
Lend me Your rope so I can climb to my highest potential,
And draw closer to You daily.

Paint my life with Your colors
Brighten my view with Your Truth
And show me what I'm blind to
Prune the dead weight off me, Lord.
All these things I ask of you in Your son's name...
Amen.

Lean on Him

You need not suffer alone…
He is with you and always has been
Even in the shadows,
The places that get no sun.
He has shone His wisdom on how to get you out of it.

When your sobs pierced the silence,
He heard you.
When you felt robbed of blessings,
He was preparing an abundance beyond your sight.
He is there!
He cares about your thoughts
Wroth-producing experiences shaking you of your last bit of faith
He wastes not on what you think you want
He's been sowing your needs before your knowledge of them.

So, you need not suffer alone
When your bones get weary of walking this road -
Let Him carry you.
This view isn't always shiny
But know there is always a divine purpose,
Beyond this moment.

I Need You Now

When unlimited seems limiting
When boundless seems binding
I'm finding myself in a pool of possibilities
Yet this one puddle of fear keeps me stuck.
So many decisions I'm becoming indecisive
And the price is…Stagnant
Immobile
The mud and murky opaqueness of the unknown is blowing my mind
Showing me I need to Pray
I need to stay on my knees and plead for a yellow brick road
Rather a green light that says "Go beyond your dreams…"
"Take a red eye and get on this early"
"Let the gray settle into black and white."
"And think about what would make your world pink again"

These sepia tones are muting my palette.
I wish to be loud again!
So, I'm shouting above, Lord
Please order my steps.
Place a border around my uncertainty.
Build a fence over my hesitance.
Restore the confidence I once had and let me run free
Let my wings release this anchor
These dank, dark corners of my questions beg of Your light, Lord
If there ever was a time… I need You now.

My Cleansing

I stepped into the waters resembling the level of setbacks I'd overcome.
Up to my waist in trials,
I gave them **all** to Him
My heart beat in anticipation,
Trepidation coupled with comfort that it'd be alright
For He has watched His child's confessions of transgressions this whole time
And said, "I still love you."

I could not shake the emotions sweeping over me.
As the last piece of my old self tried to cling on,
And was drowned by God's grace,
Waves of Peace, Gratitude and Humbling moisturized my face -
Washed over this being
And for that brief moment of submersion…
I died.

My former self was lifeless,
Laid to rest
My legs got weak, giving everything I had to this restoration
My spirit took in the full meaning before my mind did,
And my soul cried
Joyous bursts uttered the words "Thank You"
That's all I could muster…
And the only praise needed.

In my travels thereafter, I felt a calm.
A settling of debris making my footing strong,
Bringing a renewal to my focus -
Like my eyes had a film
A blurry way of viewing life - walking a path partially dim

This baptism cleansed my lenses
My vision feels HD
How mindful I am now of
Being.
Breathing.
Seeing.
And enjoying this new life He has planned for me.

The Wrong Train

Sometimes I think I might be on the wrong train.
It's had its equal shares of joys and pains but
At times I feel like the rain has surpassed an amount that is fair.
Dare I complain when my train keeps trucking along, while other peoples' songs have been cut short?
But I'm human and my sometimes ain't always
So I'll take this day to rant.
I'm always thankful but ignore the truth? I can't.

I had a plan in hand for the land I was about to explore.
I didn't sign up for what I've endured.
It had too many unbeaten trails I wasn't ready for.
Unfamiliar streets
So many occasions I wanted to retreat back to what was comfortable
Ready to accept defeat
But my Conductor Knight-Rided, auto-piloted so He could come talk to me.
Filled my tank full of faith I was gettin' low on
Gave me strength to go on.

So I relaxed, tried to enjoy the ride
Took it in stride,
Occupied myself.
Played with the cards I was dealt
And I'm wondering what kind of game am I playing?
I can't play Poker, see I've been told I'm one of a kind
So I Go Fish but I hate wishing for a match
So I'm yelling Uno to a crowded car of people that ain't playin' with a full deck
Solitaire must be my best bet, I guess, what's left?

Just my mental space filled to capacity with loneliness.
The audacity of these temporary riders
Liars leading me to believe they're strapped in 'til the final stop.
With their questionable motives - hoping to get me off track
Trying to vote me off my island but I swam back.
Inducing pollution so that my only solution is evolution
Resolution can't be one-ended, so keep it movin' is my conclusion.

This track has had so many curves and turns that I can't learn the route before it switches up on me.
I think my Conductor was testing me
Making sure the bumps didn't get the best of me
Investing values in me that I can handle anything
And with Him I can.
One split moment I tried to look past my Conductor and swore I saw a brick wall
Guess it ain't for me to see it all

This train has moved so fast that the tracks got laid down in just enough time to avoid a crash!
See even when my mind's eye is blind, my Conductor guides my path.
He lifts any unneeded weight I can't take, gets the negative freight off my train.
Cargo detrimental to my journey so that only positivity remained

Making me think perhaps this track's for me
I can't foresee the end for He holds the schedule
Allowing light at the ends of my tunnels so I'll remain hopeful.
That this isn't the wrong train, maybe just the wrong frame of mind

Lessons will be lived and learned –
Reasons will come in due time.
And so will the wisdom - this moment of clarity is important.
Illuminating my path to those who are supportive - I won't force it. The sun won't always shine through my window, but I've been equipped to adjust.
So I'll just sit back and hold tight because in Him, I trust.

Runaway Slave

My dream life is pretty active
Subtractive of true consciousness my hopes and aspirations
Freely play epic adventures on my eyelids.
Ventures into the unknown but in the home of my deepest heart thoughts,
I see what would happen if I never took a first step.
If I never soared into the upper echelon of my potential…

Apparently, I'd be a slave says my latest mindplay.
Shackled down into an abyss of mediocrity,
Bound to a sure ending,
Preventing any movement beyond consuming scraps to fulfill an undying hunger to be fed by what I truly deserve.
I'd be underserved and forever overachieving in a circle with my square-minded ideas.
I would never fit.
Fear would strike further fear with each lash,
Cracking obedience and submission into a person they wish to submerge -
39 blows attempting to bleed me out.
Blind to my unseen Lifesaver who remains above and around me.
Omnipresent hope floating me along until I decide to swim upstream.

This dream told me to Fight.
That confinement doesn't combine with my passion to live beyond and in spite of…
Beyond mistakes
In spite of shortcomings
Beyond rejection
In spite of overthinking
Beyond continual beatings

In spite of repeating self-defeating phrases that it's too hard
Beyond myself
In spite of MySelf.

I watched a fellow escapee jump to his death,
And I'm wondering if this is the half of me subliminally that wants to give up?
To surrender all efforts towards a seemingly unreachable freedom.
I considered ending the road I wasn't done paving
Then bravely looked down at what could be -
And mustered up enough resilience to do what should be.

I took this journey alone with hesitance at my back,
Resistance in the wind,
And suspense in every corner as I hid and slid past my captors,
Trappers ready with their nets investing in my stagnant future if I were ever caught.
I sought the sun to illuminate my lonely mood -
As I pursued more and more
Praying this trek would yield a harvest I've sewn seeds in long before I knew the purpose.
A deluge of trouble rushed down rapids -
Swelling vaster by the minute
Aptly resembling my self-doubt.

I swam against waves created to break my spirit,
While a voice above continued to bellow to me,
"You were made for more."
With this encouragement nourishing my thirst,
I burst through a new realm of understanding who I am -
What I am to do with this freedom.
A world of roads, forks, paths and traps lie ahead of me yet
I feel there is a beat always ordering my march
A tempo that won't let me slow down.

My Creator knew what I'd be doing before the brewings of my imagination surfaced.
So the freedom is in the discovery of who I've been this whole time…and just didn't know.
These shackles have been shades over a life meant to be brighter.
My dark thoughts colored my hope into an opaque vision that I was stuck.
Not trusting the doorknob just inches outside of my reach -
The power is Mine!

The Holy Spirit remains a divine presence I don't often tap into
And that…is an enslaved life.
A lack of knowledge to the Light I have been given if I simply reach **up** and receive.
Cleave to the power that's been within me and will be for the eternity of my existence.
He is guiding me,
Restoring me,
Imploring me to continue to move Upward and Onward.
These steps get hard but they **are** for me
Breaking down my pride with each stride into the unknown,
Oh, I know I'm being carried!
Lifted when my legs beg for solace
Rest
Just a break, Lord.
But He knows I can handle it.
Philippians 4:13 seems to whisper to me when I feel I've lost my voice.
When my chords are singed from my burning cries out into the night -
He hears me…
He steers me when my hands shield my eyes from what's coming next.

What would I do if I'd been through nothing at all?
If I didn't haul my troubles to the alter call and release them,
My appreciation of blessings would be diminished.
Finishing off entitlement with a seal of ignorance that I'm immune to pain.
He sandpapered me to my core,
Forcing me to examine the vermin determined to keep me from growing,
Eating me alive with each doubt and worry I didn't hand to Him.

The scraps made me savor the flavor of wonderful Grace.
My cold nakedness made me bask in the warmth of His Mercy.
The fear of being lynched kept me on my toes with Him holding me up -
Pushing me to break beyond my sight, even through tears.
All of these trials were necessary for me to claim victory,
And oh, how joyous it is to finally escape into His arms.

Book 2: I am Empowered.

Ode to my Sistren

Dear Beloved, I see you
I see all of you
I see your muffled cries of unhappiness,
Your constant efforts to hold broken pieces together,
The cuts bleeding you straight to your core,
How much do you have left?
Transfusing loyalty for living,
Giving parts you don't even have…
For what?
Fears keeps you buried in irrational thinking.
Tears stain the song and dance you continue to tap
Until...
Until...
You're tapped out.

But I see you
I see all of you.
My heart yearns for you to take the shades off,
Show your bruises to the world,
Let the sun of understanding shine upon the dark schema that -
You don't deserve more.
That you've reached a ceiling keeping you in this realm.
You have no idea of your potential.

But I see you.
I see all of you.
I want to give you a shovel,
A crane,
A bulldozer,
Move this mountain of shame and doubt!
Push with all your might!
Fight for yourself as hard as you fight Your Self

You too, are worth it!

If the mountain is too heavy, Beloved
Move around it.
Surround it with your bravery.
Create your peace within.
Build a dam over your waves of sorrow,
For tomorrow's a new day to stand.
And trust, I know…
I see you
I see all of you
I **am** you and outside of you.
Next to you.
Walking with you.
Together we can be -
What God has intended.

At the Corner of Wisdom and Wonder

Young girl, I see the pain behind the twinkle of hope in your eyes
The worry at the corners of your mouth
Even when you smile.
I see you hold your shoulders back against the weight you've carried in these short years.
I see the fights you've won.
I see the dreams begun and halted.
I see the steps you've taken blindly, only holding onto your faith,
And the fleeting anticipation that this will get better.

I see your breaths get short as you look at the long road ahead
Trepidation looked over your shoulder,
Attempting to break your stride.
I see your pride take a beating when you thought you had it all figured out.
I see your triggers test your growth and evolution,
And…I see you conquer it.

Young girl, strut down this path of discovery
Stand tall while you fight the two strikes you were born with
Hit a pose so hard, everyone's necks whip into Formation
Let them marvel at how you ascend oppression and stagnation
Work, Honey…
And don't ever let "them" see you blink your eyes off that prize.
It's yours, and always has been.
Just
Never.
Stop.
Walking.

Which Black/What Black

It's a shame there are days I must refrain from being as Black as I want to be
As Black as I am naturally
The Black they see superficially
The skin I am in makes others assume
My attitude is akin to someone uncivilized.
The skin I am in makes me hold in the emotion I want to express,
Suppressing my passion which can be easily misunderstood to be hood and abrasive.

I'm just tired of having to think twice about whether I'll be seen as combative or argumentative
When actually, I'm just being assertive and not allowing my voice to be muted.
Forced to put on the cute voice and diminish the bass -
So that others are not faced with fears they don't wish to address.

The questions I ask myself are agonizing
Do I want to be the straight hair Black?
The naturally-curly Black?
The bougie Black with hood tendencies Black?
The Neo-soul while still loving Hip-Hop Black?
Is it too soon to show I was born in Chester with a Coatesville flare Black?
The 'I was raised better to not show my you know what' Black?
The put my own spin on your dress code Black?
The code-switching I flip so fast I barely know I'm doing it Black?
And I sure as heck don't want to be the token Black.
The outspoken Black.
But I need to be heard Black.
So, I go back and forth about who I present today
Hoping my authenticity keeps me above water

While I'm drowning in things I never say out loud…

Because I know I'll be seen as the angry Black.
Not the knowledgeable Black!
Not the Masters-level educated Black!
Not the "my Mama raised me right" Black!
When she said I was born with 2 strikes, woman and Black…
No, no they don't see *past* the Black when something needs to be said.
Lord, please strike me dead if I'm lying -
About how much restraint it takes to be Black.

To show my pride and be forced to keep my flavor to the side.
When I'm side-by-side with people sharing the same views but a different appearance.
All they see is Black,
When I share my thoughts,
Comment on my displeasure,
File a grievance,
Get into a disagreement,
Say what I need to say with eloquence,
Give good points that are common sense.

It's this shock and surprise that I got me some good learnin'
I can see it in their eyes while their stomachs are churning
"The nerve of this Black woman!
She doesn't fit in our box!
We thoughts Afros were gone, along with French rolls and locs."
"And what is it with the changing of the hair?
Is she going to leave coconut oil residue on our chair?"

Oh, we keep them guessing, some of it has its fun
But on the other hand, I'm tired of the run.
The race between being myself and having to conform

It seems it will take decades to shift the norm.
And I just want to be me, unapologetic and strong
But if I show my true strength then I'm in the wrong...

Code-Switch This...

I am a Black woman at work.
I'm not here for play or for you to play with my hair -
Which by the way will indeed change without notice.
And nope I'm not explaining
It is all mine whether I bought it or whether it comes from my roots.

I am a black woman at work
Watch me multitask,
Get business done,
Say it all with a smile,
And walk away in 4-inch heels.

I am a black woman at work.
Now watch me work, no twerking,
Ain't nobody got time for that.
My mind is on other moves
Just watch me move...
Watch me prove you wrong.
Bust through your expectations.
Shatter your preconceived notions,
And come out shining

This black girl magic is a matchless potion
Filled with bootstraps
Busted soles
Broken hearts
Mended fences
And taped together shoelaces.
We do what we need to.
This potion will poison you if you cross us wrong

We will read, write and erase you from any remembrance of you being a factor on our radar.
It's not to be cruel -
It's just that we chose who to duel,
And what fuels our energy is Progress.
No regressions back to times we didn't have a voice.
Let me fix my crown and clear my throat...
Pass. Me. The. Glitter.

Whatever you need enhanced, we got it
No augmentation of our fly necessary
We've brought that with our DNA
And don't try to silence us with code words like 'confrontational', 'challenging' and 'opinionated'.
Just bring on the task and watch us handle it flawlessly.
With melanin glowing down the Yellow Brick Road,
Ease on down and try to duplicate this heart, brain and courage.
Probably as difficult as Goldilocks testing out that porridge,
However, we are just right.
Brown Sugar, Caramel and Mocha all sweeten the deal,
Wrapped up in protection from our ancestors -
Whose journeys have saved us a seat at the table
Labeled "Excellence Only".

See...Mediocrity won't be accepted.
We already know you're looking for any tiny misstep
Yet, this tightrope is old hat.
At this point we can manage it backwards,
We know the game.
And have achieved expert-level status
At being Queens among the masses.
Just clear a path...
And let us through.

A Scoff to a Poor Offer

She doesn't want to be an addition to your "situation".
An a la carte item,
An add-on to your already full plate.
Now, sure you can move some things to the side,
Put her in the corner until you're ready to have dessert
But she doesn't deserve this.

How insulting to her worth
This myth that she'll take anything instead of getting everything,
Not clear on what's in the water.
But please wade further to see how deep your pathology must be.
The fallacy that second place is appealing.
Don't worry, I'll wait on the confusion you're trying to intrude onto common sense.
Impose upon morals while you hibernate to catch the next in your trap.

This is exactly what's wrong with relationships…
One-on-one is replaced with 'the more the merrier' -
All because you want to share.
Or rather, be shared while she impairs her being with rejection once this all comes out.
I don't know if it's the 80/20 rule
Or the good and plenty fools that believe this is love.
I just wish I saw more examples of "normal".

Roses

This is dead and now I get roses
I suppose if this were my homegoing I'd receive a glowing bouquet from you as well.
But this has gone to hell... And I get roses?
Smelling as bittersweet as the oxymoron it is.
I love the red and pink hues and dislike you in the same line.
But that's how we always worked, isn't it?
Now that I've welcomed Genesis you have a Revelation that I was your whole world.

But Now that it has ended, I get roses?
In a clear vase as breakable as the house you threw your stones from.
Pieces get scattered when they've been shattered to dust.
Quicksand can't be picked up by any broom bare of bristles.
But, my hands come together for you…
Snaps and claps resounding from my fingertips as I pluck petals
Fretting the answer to "he loves me", "he loves me not".
I know what it is but this... Is too late.

The season has passed for these flowers to flourish
My grounds are hibernating, healing for new seeds
So, these...will last maybe a week.
Just enough time for me to have a brief weak moment
For my heart strings to ring a familiar tune
For me to remember the room you kept in my soul -
Before I cleaned shop and stopped being for Sale.

This, dear... is temporary.
As infrequent as the "I love you"s.
As barren as the emotional expression unless it was the fury.

Any jury would say you are guilty of tap-dancing when the curtains have closed so,
I hear you... I just can't see you.
Just as I can no longer see you as my future.

The sutures to my heart barely had any stitches left to -
have and hold the love of another
So, I left in just enough time.
Before I was completely devoid of any growth,
Frozen like the tundra in Siberia.
Theories have contended I like the sun much better.
The beams refresh my dreams of brighter tomorrows forevermore
So, this may be slightly impressive
Yet not progressive to the path I've chosen
I've freshly rewoven my reward pathways, so I'm not weirdly addicted to pain,
Acclimated to disappointment,
Surprised by joy,
Imagine that...

The web was so tangled it that right angles looked round
That silence was the best sound I ever heard.
So, I will dance to my heart beating lighter.
Let new butterflies tickle the corner of my mouth.
I shall look at these roses as a moment in time.
A reminder that everything is great in its prime,
Yet will die if not nurtured and cherished...
If not treated as richly as their first bloom,
Even when the pinks and reds fade.
So, this...has had its run but I'm ready to let go
Throwing the last flower 6 feet below
As this phase of my life descends to peacefully rest
With this rose, I bid thee Adieu.

The Sun Setting on Hope

Every man knows the moment she lost that look in her eyes.
The twinkle that's gone,
Star-crossed saucers look like empty plates that -
Used to be so full of hope and fulfilling promise.
Now only a few stray crumbs left,
A reminder of what used to be,
And he used to be eager to give her what she wants.
Now he scoffs at those same gestures
The pressure of keeping things fresh has fizzled out,
Flat on top of ice cream,
Never having a chance to float again.

The boat descends down a cliff of white water rapids
Crafted to destroy even the strongest foundations.
But this one was always shaky…
Constructed on the San Andreas Fault,
Put out a recall on the manufacturing of this operation,
The company should declare bankruptcy.

Because what she sees is all tinted brown.
The sun shines in sepia at high noon.
The full moon cries rusted tears -
Fears shining brighter to be stifled by unpredictable storms.
So, the norm is… Muted.
Strong chords struggle to whisper.
Her voice soars in her mind's ears,
Bellowing regret and reasons why the push and pull had appeal,
Revealing uneven footing,
A rickety see-saw,
And she saw way too much for the twinkle to return.
Retinas burned out by fiery lies,
An inferno of deception singed her pupils and blackened her soul.

Leaving questions like would she ever be whole again?

The holes are so big.
As big as her eyes fighting tears,
Blinking back pain suppressed,
Regressing to the little girl who never thought love hurt.
But this has eclipsed almost all hope,
Of her eyes dancing to love's melodies,
Of her heart prancing to love's drum,
Of a chance to hear the syncopation of unity -
Manifested in a new blessing nestling in her womb.

Yet the room is empty and so are her eyes…
Darkened by unmet expectations.
Glazed over by waiting for change,
Dried out by staring ,
Glaring and waiting for a new answer to old sh…
Even old hits can be remixed but wow,
It's just not there.
Like washing dishes in old water, it's just not the same
Like praying for rain in her last breath,
She doesn't have anything left.

So, her eyes wave the flag at half-mast.
Mourning the aspirations of anything further.
Surrendering to many battles, wars and tours around a world of failed compromises -
But, no more.
The only trips down memory lane will be reminders of lessons
Past regressions where she suppressed her needs
But, no more!

No cure for the toxicity he bore into her lenses.
No score for a lose-lose situation.

No getting the red out for clear eyes -
That simply mask a much-needed cleanse.
No more bending to levels that should have been surpassed long ago.
It's time to grow, heal and move on.
Rest these eyes barely staying open,
Broken vessels showing the strain,
Painfully dying one blink at a time.
It's time for them to close…
Restore what was lost,
And awaken with a clear perspective.

Book 3: I am Enlightened.

The Cost of Sight

There is so much that I could write.
So much building inside of me that I am silent.
I am mute on an abundance of feelings, emotions and experiences.
I am entranced by things that pass my eyes,
Pierce my ears,
Break my skin,
Enter in and stay trapped.
It's not that I have nothing to say…
It's that I am chronicling the importance of my prose.
The priority of my attention.
My intent to bend language with purpose and progress
My process is… mine.
No rushing the production of my innermost thoughts.

I see it all…
And I am careful with my delivery,
Cautious with my vulnerability,
Protective of my sharing,
Caring about how the message is received,
Preparing my heart to bleed publicly.
Wondering if my words fall in an empty room…
Do they make a sound?
Or rebound on ears not ready for the truth.
Reverberating on halls of desperate echoes buried in souls lost to the life.
To the strife endured,
To the plight I'm sure has singed the fabric of multiple generations.
Relationships intertwined in lies and deceit,
Defeat screaming through mothers' tears,
Desperation oozing through the pores of tough skin.
Oh, I see it all…
I see them fall and I do my best to pick them up -

As I reattach fragments of my heart that shatter -
With each story I hear.

It's not that I have nothing to say…
It's that I pray to God my hands can hold yet another tragic picture framed in flames engulfing the innocence of our youth,
Pondering if this is the intervention that extinguishes their pain-…
at least temporarily. Leaving them a glimmer that the past and present doesn't have to be their future.
But, I hear it all…
I see them fall down stairs they know like the back of their hand.
Blinded by systems set up to fail them -
Impale them of their bootstraps,
Puppeteer them into submission,
The provisions are meager and systems are so eager to point the finger.
I see hands so ashy from washing away sorrows with liquor and drugs.
I see rugs bulging with mounds of dirt that everyone steps around.
I see shaky grounds breaking from constant pressure,
And I see fingers pointed.
Questioning who's responsible for the cleanup.
I, for sure, have a lot to say…
It's bottled up because if I start, I will never stop.
My voice would lose effect.

The woes I expose will sound like a squeaky wheel -
While I'm striving to heal my approach,
Their pain,
And I how I process it all,
So, I am mute…

Until the distress presses up against my lips and I must roar
Until I need to pour out all that I take in,
Allowing my breaking point to just bend.
I need that relief so that I can be a link,
And think about what to do next…

For What do we Zoom

We live fast,
Drive fast,
Buy fast.
Not sure how long our lives are going to last.
The expectancy doesn't rest in normalcy
Instead we dwell as outliers,
Crying when we make it past the bell curve.
Our standard deviation is the creation of this hatred based on our melanin.
It puts us in these intricate decisions where we
Live fast
Drive fast
And buy fast.
Try to have something that lasts beyond this dash.

This space between birth and death gets more shallow -
As people's sanity jumps off the deep end.
The more we drown in despair,
The more we want to drip in ice without a care for tomorrow.
It's all borrowed…
On a lender.
And we can't depend on rules and regulations to keep us safe,
So, our security Rests. In. the Peace. of having stuff.
Who cares about the fluffy meaning of materialism?
The never-ending game of brand names,
Popping tags and what not ,
Hell, we're just trying not to be another hashtag…

Therefore, we brag about what we have in the here and now.
Flash and flicker now or forever be held to tricky guidelines that -
only match for people resembling the paper it's written on.

This song is tired...
I'd love to retire my bitterness,
Receive a pension for all the work I put in,
Yeah, it's not seen the same.
Minimal gains for double the hurt
Damn right I'm gonna buy this new shirt.
It might be the one I'm staying in when I'm buried in dirt...
These days you just never know.
So, I have optimism on one shoulder and realism on the other,
Let them duke it out for a while
While my emotions recover -
From the confusion of just waking up and surviving
The elation of arriving home...whole.

So, for now…
Until the record stops stalling on the part where we are skipped over.
I'm going to -
Live fast
Drive fast
Buy fast.

Choking on Commercialism

The nooses have 2 chainz.
The whips gleam down the streets reflecting immediate gratification,
Frivolous spending instead of investing in something worthwhile -

All the while we say we're oppressed
But we seal the envelope sending us into a myriad of excuses.
Useless statements crying wolf -
Yet Wall Street isn't that far.

It just that we are confused on who keeps us down.
We're down for the cause making us wanna holler -
To the choir who already knows the same song.
How long will we use our lungs?
Our breath on complaints regarding why we're on the same rung of the ladder -
No matter how far we've come.
Lenny still wanna sell jewelry out of his jacket.
We praise the ratchet for our entertainment.
Kanye called it crack music;
I call it a hemorrhage.
Self-inflicted bruises like the crazy lady from Thin Line between Love and Hate.
Because that's exactly what it is…
A thin line between on time and late
And we love CP time.
But wait...

Our energy is exhausted into faulty reasoning
It's like our wiring needs remodeling.
We're modeling after what we know.
So, the smokescreen is that we can't help it -
But let it be a whip,

Or a chain,
And we're ready to hang ourselves willingly on whatever's fresh and new
Beat the crowd to be the first to cop it
So, who's to blame?

Sorrowful Palm Readings

Their hands could relieve a hurt.
Yet they use them to birth hatred.
Breed continual harm.
Yield angst among their brothers.

Their hands could serve to pull another to the finish line.
Cut the tape leading to a world of possibilities.
Clasp fingers around the installation of hope,
But they tighten the rope around their own necks.
Struggling to breathe new solutions,
Choking on force-fed pills that they are not better than this.
Who told them this?
Was it the hand that fed them?
The hand that never adjusted the chalk so they could hear above-
The screeching cries that they'll never be anything?
Was it the hand that beat insecurity in their walk?
So, they stalk around the bottom,
Feeding into half-truths

The mass cruelty I see staining my screen,
Careening into a normalcy where hands represent
Pain.
Blood.
Death.
I wish they knew what else their hands could do…
They could sow seeds and reap their harvest.
Lord, if they only knew they were made for more.

Social Shackles

I see so many people out here hitting the search button.
It's like as soon as it was easier to become closer virtually-
It made it harder to connect.
So, we hit all these keys hoping it will please others,
And feed us what we are empty of.
Except when they don't hit the like key or the love key,
We feel **we** are unlovable.
The virtual hugs aren't enough and all we want is to be touched.

So, we keep going.
We keep blowing God's work,
And alter....
And contort...
And bend to fit in to standards deemed unreasonable.
Please like me,
Please love me,
Please hug me…from over there.
Do you care that I took 20 of these photos hoping one would be perfect?
Hoping you would love it?
And that tiny heart would be all I needed for mine to keep beating
For me not to feel like defeat won again.
Because finally you saw me in the way I wanted to present-
Resenting the insides of me that no one will understand.

So, please receive this outside as my best.
Dig deeper if you wish but the picture ain't pretty.
Here I am…
Please like me,
Please love me,
Please hug me!
This media isn't social at all.

It's actually isolating,
Antisocial to reality.
This fluff pads us from the hard knocks,
The hard rocks that get thrown attempting to shatter our character.
Not knowing our worst critic does its best work.
The critiques are just cutting a few recently applied stitches,
But do your best...
Here I am.
Please like me,
Please love me,
Please hug me.

Coming Now...Nonsense

I'm exhausted by the multitude of CNN updates.
It's starting to feel like "Coming Now...Nonsense".
When will it mean something that makes me smile?
Instead of confusion and disbelief over our current position in this existence.
By happenstance and no coincidence that our indecisive approach left us divided...
And now we are united in regret, shame and guilt.
Anything built is being broken down by a toddler with too much power-
And plenty of toys to destroy us.

Coming now... Nonsense.
Maybe if the tweeting ceased, we would believe there was actual progression of favorable ideals,
As opposed to made-up words and phrases less smart than a fifth-grader.
I can't eat anymore deception.
I can't see another verbal tantrum.
I can't bear witness to the twisted visions blind to reality.
I'm counting the days until perhaps this division improves.
Until we collectively join to be smart about our futures.

I'm bleeding out fear,
Exhaling disgust,
And when I sigh it's because I have nothing else to say...
Then my phone lights up again.
Coming Now, Nonsense is at it for another round of "Who's Lie is it Anyway?", and this game is tired.
Nothing's funny.
Plenty of scenarios running in my mind where this doesn't end-well.

Maybe *this* is hell.

Where is "better"?
How come the weather isn't changing?
This social climate is near equator heat.
Scorching our melanin like the lynchings burned into our history.
The backwoods mentality is daily front-page reporting,
While our retorting at the forecast continues to lose its volume.
I presume we could only go up from "here"
But with Coming Now, Nonsense persistently in our ear,
It's hard to tune out the noise-
And poise ourselves to endure.
To find a frequency that resounds with our heartbeat's narrative.
'Tis a blaring shift from what we intended.
Like a train hurtling towards a fork with 2 dead ends…
Maybe *this* is Hell.

Yet, my soul won't allow me to commiserate but so much.
The humor enveloped in this ridiculousness keeps me in touch with my inner child.
The little girl with Promise beyond proof,
Faith despite of fear,
And Hope overpowering helplessness.

Coming Now, Nonsense will continue to saturate my screen-
However, my maturation towards my highest Self,
Keeps me elevated above the chatter.
Knowing all that matters are my actions, reactions
And how I use my voice.
So, my choice is to mute the noise,
Dim the screen,
Ascend,
And shine bright.

One Step. One Voice.

We need…one beat.
One sound.
One rhythm.
One march.
All of these agendas straying from the purpose-
To be seen…
We are Here.
Can you hear us, Horton?
We are Here.

We are crying,
Prying our eyelids open for the next day.
Hoping for a better result that doesn't say-
Anything about acquittals when the facts are clear.
We are Here.
Can you hear us, Horton?
We are Here.

Our insides are out,
Bleeding on the ground.
We are stomping in our pain,
Hoping you hear the sounds of our souls…
Weeping, pleading with the unreasonable,
The unbearable,
The unfair advantages of our oppressors.
Heaps of stressors piled on and weakening our hearts,
Clogging our arteries,
And choking us of a full voice decree
WE. ARE. HERE!

We will never stop saying it.
Never stop praying it.

Tattooing it on our throats-
With no problem going hoarse.

We know you see us as this tiny speck.
But took a liking to our style and stole it,
Trying to keep in step.
However misguided your plight, oh greedy one,
You forget we originated the drum.
That the grooves in the dirt were birthed by our weary feet.
Crossing the sands into a land ironically intended for freedom,
Yet swindled from hesitant owners.

You've shown nothing but ignorance.
A stance clearly undermining our agenda.
A potent blend of veiled rhetoric and enough checks to balance this increasing deficit of common sense-
And humanity
Yet…we are Here.
Lowering the volume isn't in our blood.
Bring on the flood of tyrant-tinged tantrums
Our resilience is measured by how hard we've been beaten into the ground.
We bounce back just as high into your world of fantasy and fallacy.
I know you hear us…
Trust you will hear all instruments synchronized into one sonic-
Boom.
Where there will be no room remaining for excuses.
We are Here.
Can you hear us, Horton?
We
Are
Here.

Book 4: I am Loving.

Manifesting Destiny

Some people really are Still Dreaming-
And I'm one of them.
Ton of stems and roots I'm trying to ground,
Sprinkle water on,
So I can have the Tree I believe in.

I'm still dreaming-
Of the day when I don't overanalyze,
Just realize it's gonna be what it is.
But what it is, is always less than what I want,
Because I'm still dreaming of ultimate happiness.
Wondering if it really exists-
Or just exists in storybooks,
Overlooked by the reality of true life.

But I'm Still Dreaming…
Day and night-
About my knight in shining armor that will let me relax.
While he does it all,
Or half, hell I'll take it,
Work with it,
Own it,
Make it mine,
We can both shine in this dream.
Beam the good vibes from the both of us
Like Captain Planet,
Make a better world for us-
In God we Trust.

But I'm Still Dreaming…
Even though my leaves get worn down,
Fall off,

The spring always sings a new light.
That bright green refreshes the part of me that gets-
Rusted by the cold winter of people's hearts and intentions,
Withered by trying with no results or resolutions.

But I'm Still Dreaming...
Seems like I should sleep more, huh?
Get it right.
My true sight is blinded by fears,
Some predated, some more created.
But my dreams come with such sincerity and clarity-
That it's making me think Nyquil may be the quick fix,
Sick or not.
Not to hide from reality-
But it does bite right now.
Not much left of the apple I shared,
Insides getting brown,
Chewed up by some unassuming souls-
That thought the shiny red exterior was the total picture.
But wait...there's more!!

Because I'm still dreaming...
Never stopped.
Never clocked in or out.
I'm ever evolving,
Reaching.
Striving,
To have exactly what I want.

Got more than a few grains of sand left in my life-glass
To make my dream last forever-
Just have to get it together.

Whenever I dream, the hope shines so bright.

Like the rain that changes its mind,
And lets the sun play just a little bit longer…
How nice.
The price is just not a penny for my thoughts.
I've brought my best visions to the table-
Praying that someone will be able to get it.
Get me.
Get the dream of course,
That's all I talk about, right?
But I can't let it go…

The path I have mapped out is invaluable-
Infallible for the right pair.
We just both have to yearn to be "There".
It's unfair for one to dream and the other to be in-
A stagnant fragment of still space,
Especially when I see so much potential.

So, I keep dreaming
Of **complete** congruence,
Without outside influence,
Opinions on stuff they know nothing about,
Trying to convince that another branch is the way.
It's okay to be the only ones standing…
Someone has to start,
Put their hand out,
And build up the ones around them.
Blaze a trail that leads to more than-
Tripping before the finish line is in sight.
Starting yet another race with a DQ.

It's true that some people really are content with inaction.
But not even a fraction of me can sit still,
And let bliss skip by on its merry way,

That's why every day I'm still …

I had some people in my life that tried to stop my dream,
I'm not having it.
Tried to gleam in the falsehood of smoke and mirrors-
I'm not laughing.
I love Langston but this will not be a dream deferred…
I overheard a little birdie saying this is **my** time,
Our time,
The right time to not look back.
Rejoice over the lessons learned and move the hell on…
And on and on.
My cipher keeps moving not by the beats of others-
But by my own internal metronome.
Ticking tockin' til ya don't stop.
Pop lockin' my way to "betterness".
My past was a mess-
As abstract as Vincent,
And since then it's been back to stick figures.

I figured out it's easier to keep it simple,
And if you can't get with that-
You know what to do.
Don't wake me ,Chris said…
Don't try to break me down to keep me in your nightmare.
Shaking me isn't going to change anything.
I don't care what you do.
I just took an Ambien and I'm only in my first hour of rest
So, do your worst. Hell, do your best!
But final hour tap dancing will never work for me.

Took me too long to hang the picture on the wall just right.
So, I'll be damned if anyone ties a rope around my cloud nine-
It's not moving.

In fact, it's stuck…
…on trust, faith and a little bit of luck.
Glued in the sky by sweet honey memories
And more to come…

So like Annie I sure did,
Bet my bottom dollar,
Put my last quarter in the slot ,
Spent my complete life savings on that horse,
Of course (of course) I did.
All for my eternal craving of just one final blink of shut eye,
Hoping that it won't deny me any piece of my vision.

So, I'm living for the day where-
My Rapid Eye Movement pays off-
Due to progress and improvement of my never-ending dream.
Working towards the moment where it seems I was awake the whole time,
But until then I'm still…

Letter to my Future Husband

I want our worlds to align,
Combust into a wonderful combination of what makes us glow.
Circles crossing,
Overlapping our qualities while fine-tuning our flaws so our chords harmonize
Compliment the lows with a melody we sing even when we feel muted.

I wish to name a new star that reflects our unique language.
Words with meanings we keep close to our hearts,
Impermeable to slick approaches the masses elevate,
I want to be grounded with you.
Spiritually.
Emotionally.
Physically.
I want our centers to meet intimately where we miss each other immediately after our love song is played…
…And replayed.

I want to lay my fears on your chest.
Bare my soul to you and have you clothe me in your security.
Your strength where my hesitance has no home in our cocoon-
For I want you to give me room to spread my wings,
Knowing I will always find you-
Love you.

Never losing sight of your goals, I'll be sure to support you, Love.
Concretely bolstering the desires of your heart,
Be not afraid to plant your flower here.
I'll water your thoughts when your doubts drought you of any hope.

I'll remove your weeds of negativity when the world beats your creativity.
Let me tend to you, Love.

If you need shade from the rays of pressure,
Burning a hole in you that seems inescapable,
Allow me to cool you with my calm.
I have plenty of lemonade with the mess I've been given, Baby
Let me share my solace with you.
Help you find your peace within when the world is loud,
Let's be quiet together.
I want only our hearts to hum soft, soothing sounds to each other-
Creating bonds wrapping ribbons around our weaknesses.

I want to make you better and you do the same for me.
I want every part of us that unites to ignite fire.
Passion.
Explosive waves of joy glazing over us,
Covering the tart pieces we share only with one another-
I want life to be sweet.
Complete with communication emanating understanding even when we don't speak.
I wish to learn your dark side-
And not judge you for keeping it hidden.
They didn't understand you, but I make my vow to you-
That each day I'll peel back whatever layers you let me.
I know you can't forget your past hurts,
But may I please be your first-aid?
Your first responder when it all falls down,
Let me catch you, my Love.

No triangles in a 2-person circle,
My geometry ain't never been great so I like to keep it simple.
Let me be the shortest distance to your peace…

All these things I ask of you because I know I will give them to you without question.
Yet, I reckon this is all premature-
Because I don't know who you are.
But I will continue to be who I am… until…
God brings you to me.

Daybreak after Darkness

Good morning, Love
I didn't think we'd see each other so soon after the deep night of darkness we had.
But I can say I'm happy to see you brightening the suns of my tomorrows.
How stellar you shine when my lines defining lonely vs. alone-
Had just recently dried on walls God helped me rebuild when I lost him.
And here you come knocking on my door like you were just on vacation for awhile,
While placating my insecurities that you were gone forever.

How have you been, Love?
I feel like we need to catch up over International Foods coffee so I can tell you what I've been through,
When I was pretty sure despair was my side piece.
See, you be playin' with me but this last time you really snatched yourself away.
You stole into the night and finished me.
Taking my soul and hope in one last breath-
Leaving me gasping for deliverance from this pain.

But Love…I saw glimpses of you here and there,
In the star's twinkles,
And the laughter of children.
Hidden between healing and heartache,
Buried in the bosom of the desire to be pleasantly surprised.
My eyes spotted you in the corners when you thought I wasn't looking.
I felt you watching me…
Assessing whether I was ready for your return-
And ready or not, here you are.

Licking my wounds and pruning off my resentment of you.
I'd offer you a chair but don't you **dare** take it if you don't plan on settling in for a while,
And basking in the full spectrum of my smile when you actually treat me right.
That's right. I said it…

How can I forget your wayward wind that swept me into blissful ignorance?
I'm working on my bitterness but please allow me to crawl,
Then walk into my sea legs,
While your vessel slashes through my murky doubt.
I'm not proud of the walls I built but when you left me with sand…
My tears were the glue that built this castle of resilience.

Forgive me if I don't show my hand all at once.
I've gotten so crafty at bluffing that I can slip a Queen past a trifecta of high spades.
Please don't play with me this time.
Just once…
Let Us beat Them.

Hesitantly Speaking...

I want-
I want to tell him that I ....
My heart's been secretly speaking to his for some time now
But won't allow me
To reveal this fact vocally.
Why have fear of something so great?
Can't let it get too late before my lips forget how to part.

Where should I start?
These words can never be taken back once I break the seal of freedom.
My heart is imploding with the anticipation of emotions unheard.
Such powerful words,
Yet I feel powerless.
Slave to my own experiences,
Shackled by repeated instances when I was there-
And he was not....
And my outgrown vest couldn't protect me
From the heart-breaking shots of
Silence....
Distance...
And awkward space.

Maybe,
Just maybe this time,
I won't have to erase the half-drawn pictures and start over.
My supplies are getting low,
Resources coming in slow,
No telling how much more I can go
before I need help holding my arms up.
Maybe...

Just maybe this time
We can go half on the canvas.
He brings the paint,
I have the brushes-
And we can fumble around life's trials and error,
And complete each other as much as two lost souls can manage-
Slowly lifting the fog of stifling pain.
Hopefully some sun is left in us…
Make a pretty picture for once.

No secret that I am literally scared speechless.
Rendered a mute on life's greatest subject.
Foundation of all creations,
God's everlasting gift…
And I can't share
Can't say it
Can't even write it
Sh**.
What can lift this?

If the words reached me first….
Oh my dry, cracked heart has a yet to be quenched thirst for the moisturizing relief-
That I am more than capable of touching his soul-
In the same way he erased my resistance to being touched at all.

My lips are going to betray me soon….
I can feel it.
I put my all into the goodnight kiss,
To stifle it.
Shut it up for as long as I can while I wait….
And wait…
I feel fake not being true to this unmistakable reality.

Purgery is a crime and I don't have much more time on the stand
Before another witness unleashes the lines-
I've been trying to mask as undefined.
But why?
Everyone knows but him.

I know he feels me…
Baby, please feel me.
Hold my hand and guide me through-
While I try to clear up and swim through
The murky existence of the unknown….

The Throb of Yearning

I long for you too...
My body aches and anticipates your return to my embrace.
My heart races thinking about the rush your presence brings me.
I can feel your sweetness pulse through my veins.
Surges of passionate remembrances that you were right next to me.
It's as if you take my exhale when you exit so...
I inhale deeply searching for your scent in my sheets.

Craving to be rejuvenated,
I roll around attempting to soak up your essence.
I swallow my pride as I admit your impact has enveloped me in a euphoria I'd be heartbroken if halted.
And this is nowhere near the peak or apex of what I feel for you.
It's just the only truth I can actually speak words upon.
For the rest is this known, felt, spiritual experience that verbs and nouns would ruin.
All I know is...I'm yours.

The doors and pathways to this bliss are a road only you've traveled
I've had my hand out for what seems to be an eternity,
Losing firm holds with shaky fingertips,
Yet with you I can securely grip onto my innermost dreams
And believe
...it can be.

Is It Okay?

With questions swirling,
Twirling new experiences in my mind,
Like my favorite cream in my coffee,
Warming my insides as you do,
And calming my tides as only you can
I need to know...
Is it okay to be in love with you now?

The timing and things left undefined,
Minding my needs as if you are more than what you are...
So far I'm loving my heartbeat's staccato.
And songs that stick in my head describing you.
And so much you give me by simply being you.
Being true to your words and truer to your heart,
So I wonder if I'm ahead of myself-
Or mindfully ahead of what I already know will be
Will we feel this way ...forever?

Whether it's the now or the here we may be in a year's time
I can no longer hide from what my insides are screaming to you.
It's wise to silence this in the midst of my touch and kiss
And hope you hear me out.
Please read my sighs between the lines and cries to you that
I never and I mean never have been so affected...
Reflecting back on the past trips to Oz
I never knew where I was going and neither did they.
They were missing crucial pieces that would have left me dead if I gave it.
A brain refraining from constant ridicule
A heart full of unconditional giving
The courage to say any of this.
Yet you are filling my chalice to the brim-

Making me marvel at how good Home feels.
Sipping, simmering me down as emotions boil over-
You receive them all.
Not questioning my mindplay bouncing around life's pinball machine,
Hoping I have one more life left to try again and actually win.
To actually think I can have all that I put in.
The joy output is immeasurable,
Pleasurable sensations overtake my psyche-
And this might be the best feeling I've ever...
Is it okay to say this now?

I'm done arm-wrestling this blissful revelation,
Elation washes over any fears I have of jumping over the moon and shouting from the stars-
That this constellation was written before we ever realized.
Pieces of the sun shine in my eyes when I gaze at a rarity such as you...
Your touch tickles fantasies,
Plans that we could do this for more than a reason or a season-
But to have all this in me now...
I'm scared.

The barriers make more than complete sense,
But my heart doesn't listen and when you touch Her core,
She loses all logic.
Loses all grips on reality...
Fingertips slipping off deliberate intention,
Splashing into waves lacking any prevention of making premature moves.

Dare we float without an oar to shores of unlimited passion?
Crash into once barren islands of disappointment and build from there?

Bare our souls' fears and walk around naked without shame?
Share our tears into a cup filled with promise,
Letting that quench our overflowing desire for each other.
Will you soothe the rough edges of my hesitance?
Erode uneven patches until we melt into each other seamlessly?
I beg thee please stay with me on the edge of vulnerability.
Hold my hand as I gaze over the cliff.
Rifts and ripples of blue caressing the rocks-
As I address these blocks in my mind.
The water looks so lovely and welcoming,
Like the fountain of youth erasing the bittersweet nectar of truth delighting my taste buds-
I feel renewed.

My fire red mood blends with your mellow yellow
We glow copper and watch our suns set in a view so breathtaking-
You wish time would slow down to catch every hue.
We burst into rainbows,
Bellowing joyous melodies blending into an unrehearsed harmony.
Even our hums sing notes we could boast reach octaves uncharted
Your bass clef hooks me into a groove so moving,
Swaying me in rhythmic beats such that
I could dance on you all night.
My only fright is...is this stance too soon?

The chance to swoon and fan myself comes often
Even in an empty room, your impression on me is jarring
For you to have a starring role in what I hold so close to me is…
I certainly don't mind
I just find myself fighting my words
So contradictory to who I am
And I wish to save some things for the moment where we put a dead bolt on this lock and key that already fits so securely-
Closing the door to any permeations,

Invasions from others that envy even our beginning.
My wheels are spinning at the infinite possibilities of us,
But I trust the pace.
The space we've placed between us and around us-
Allowing our untouched meadows to be tended and tilled until…

I will continue to let them cultivate and grow.
For now, please allow all non-verbals to be the absolute truth.
And if our paths bring us "here" one day…
There will be a lot I need to tell you.

He Is My...

He is my...
No one word can describe the volume and magnitude of his meaning to me
So, I see it necessary to express the depths of his
imprint stamped on my heart.

He is my...
unlimited joy enveloped in brown skin
and a grin that melts the frozen parts of me.

He is my...
heart's desires manifested in a surreal reality
moving me to ponder whether I am actually awake.

He is my...
every boundless dream imaginable yet finally within my reach
teaching me to forever strive for infinite possibilities
and never settle.

He is my...
rhythm in my strut, wind in my hair
for he makes me feel light
like I'm traveling on a butterfly's wings.

He is my...
song I sing effortlessly and flawlessly
for the beauty is in the passion of the melody
not in the precision of being perfect.
I hit notes loud and right because he sees the best in me.

He is...
my radiant smile at the silliest things.

He is…
my hips moving to the harmony we create in silence.

He is…
more than a friend though such a foundation created this very moment.

He is…
not my boyfriend for this is a Man
in every sense of the word.
From his maturity to his integrity
to the way his stride reflects wisdom in his young years.
A walk that evokes tears
by just the sheer knowledge of the hills and valleys he's endured.
I see so much in store for

He is my…
vision I never dared to share with anyone else
for their sight was blinded by doubt and fear
but here he and I are and it's so hard to know what to call him.

I just know he is my…
Happiness in the staccato of my heartbeat
when his presence shines over my past pain
I will no longer refrain from calling him my…
Strong climax of multiple emotions
washing refreshing waves over my eroded hope.

He is my…
unlocked and untapped bliss
Breaking chains that had me rooted
in a cloudy existence.

He is my…
Clarity in simplicity.
My…Honesty with delicate delivery.
My…Gentleness in the eye of the storm.
For our climate is peaceful
no matter the seasons we encounter.
We even dance in the rain
appreciating God's droplets that
leave our souls renewed and ready to conquer any challenge.

He is my…
twinkle in these dark brown eyes
taking in this unhindered view with new lenses.

He is my…
provider of emotional safety.
My…supporter of individuality.
My…safe space to just BE.
Hence, my hesitation in naming him
is not a minimization of his importance.
I deem it the complete opposite
for it is a reflection
an introspection
a pause in my inability to be concise.
My life is and will forever be shifted by this…
By him.
Where I can only find presumptuous comfort in simply calling him
…my Future.

A Pause in Time

I want the moment
I want time to stand still for this precious pause,
And I want to feel everything climax in those minutes and seconds that go by.

I want this day not to feel like any other day-
Nothing ordinary about the time you set the tone for the rest of our lives.
I want…the moment.
An apex of emotion that chronicles our time spent together
So much that I have no choice but to say
"Yes".

I don't wish to be neglected of the element of surprise.
I want your eyes to lock on me and seal the security of our bond.
I want my safety to finally rest in the warmth of your forever embrace.
I need my questions to end, when you ask yours…
I see the door of our future just outside of our reach
So, when you speak this inquiry of matrimony,
Be ready for the fast and furious tears,
Rapidly rushing down my face,
Remembering the years I've waited for those words to tickle my ears.
And how sweet the sound of your voice delights my fancy.
Please, take your time my Love…

Let our story unwind in the visions of your mind
As you rewind our first kiss and reminisce about the surge of passion-
That made you want to purge your soul to me.
Tell me about the shift in space and time

Where our worlds aligned,
And you saw me being a part of every piece until we die.
Show me the blank slate where you erased your fear,
Once I appeared,
Moving you to take this leap with me,
Allowing me to co-author our unique recipe.

A brew that has our best flavors enhancing each other's palette-
And expanding upon what we thought love should be.
But we, my love…created our own harmony,
Didn't we?
Tuned into a higher vibration
Bellowing above ordinary and soaring into an echelon of bliss.
This is us…
I trust you've calculated the tics and tocks that rocked us into this unbelievable dream,
One that we never thought was possible until now.
How bemusing this clock has been…
I blinked and suddenly my heart beat your name
You colored my shades of gray and painted a masterpiece of exactly what I wanted.
You simplified my complicated equations by merely adding yourself in-
So, there is no doubt that a subtraction of you would equal a lesser me.
Like chemistry, when our elements bonded
I was never the same again,
Nor do I wish to be.
My answer will leave no guesses.
The universe has already blessed our union.
Hence, please assume my reply to your request will be resounding
I will…I do…
I love you now.
And will…forevermore.

Nudity of the Soul

He stripped me
Emotionally naked
Vulnerable and exposed.
He unclothed my self-doubt
Made space for my flaws
And loved me for all of them.
He bandaged my mistakes
And showed me his for me to tend to.
We traded war stories and marveled
At how far we'd come.

For once, emotionally naked felt freeing
I danced around in my new skin
Revealing shortcomings openly
Knowing they'd be received non-judgmentally,
Lovingly and without conditions-
This position felt....right.

Previously I held tight to my ugly side
Doubting anyone would be able to-
Accept my dark and light.
Yet he met me in the heaviest of downpours,
And told me the sun was just ahead if we walk a little more.

What a love I knew.
What joy I felt.
I melted at simplicities…
I breathed in appreciation ,
And with each exhale I sighed
Gratitude.

Liberated Harmony

Free.
Free to be me.
Free to be you.
Free to be we.
Together we can grow without limits and with us in it
Our possibilities are infinite.

We are free to explore
Unopened doors
Untraveled roads
Free to explode inside each other.
Breaking out of this confined box
With meaningless locks and rules on how we should
Do this thing called Newness.

We are free to build on the rubble of our troublesome pasts-
Hapless attempts at a vibe we find to be effortless.
We are free to live and learn from life's lessons
And there no guessing that we've both been through some messes.
Me thinking he was the one when it was only fun
You thinking she was it when it was bullsh**.

But we are free to be wise and know that
Naivete will not be our demise.
Free to realize our lives were placed in this moment-
Right on time.
Like an unexpected surprise you secretly hoped for in the back of your mind.
Like a random act of kindness when you were at the brink of madness.
We are free to redefine happiness.
Free to expose our deepest vulnerabilities-

And know they will be met with equal insecurities,
Because being free is scary.
This newness has mystery,
And we both have histories we don't wish to repeat.
But we are free to complete each other-
In a way no other can compete.

Free to support
Free to seek comfort in each other's arms
Like a lost child in a world full of harm.
Free to get it right this time.
Free to be wrong sometimes!
Free to understand that time is on our side.

Free to control this train of refreshed hope-
Coping with mistakes we're bound to make,
But knowing this strong bond, they will not break.
Free to express what was previously suppressed
Resting on no less than complete honesty and respect ,
Blessed to take on any critic's test.

Free to release ourselves,
Break out of the shells,
From the virtual hells we've both fallen victim to….
But this ain't the time to dwell,
Because we are finally free to awaken each other's senses
Like freshly cut lenses to the visually impaired.
We can share this new vision, that shall only be hidden-
To those with inhibitions.
But having limits is not what being free is about….

So, let's shout this freedom song

Bringing anyone along,
Who wants to travel and unravel themselves,
From the packaging of cookie-cutter courtship.

I'm free to admit I don't have all the answers,
But I'm willing to take a chance on you.
If you'd just take a glance at the beginning I've envisioned—
Perhaps add your own lines,
May be the best story ever written…
Scripted by two beings on a daunting journey to be
Unlimited
And refreshingly
Free.

Book 5: I am Sensual.

Dimly-Lit Caresses

As the candlelight flickers I get a flash
Images of us exploring each other's minds.
Unwinding tangled pasts into straight lines of-
Simplicity, warmth and attraction.
Playful touches tickle our minds' fancies.
Glances ponder what could be,
And in that moment, I was happy to be-
Here.
Next to you.
Comfort rises to complete openness where-
Only shyness is forbidden.
And hidden behind my eyes is an intense je ne sais quoi,
Yet I do know my heart's song.

The glances long to tell you much.
So, I touch with deep intention
Process feelings unmentioned with each knead and rub…
Rhythmic caresses express unbridled desires and care-
And I wish you to allow me to care for you.
Attend to tight areas of mind and body as long as you need.
Please let me talk to you in this way without any interruption…

Please let me trace upon those deep scars
and hear the story behind them.
Open the door and let my curiosity explore-
the room you shield to most.
Offer me a seat into your intensity,
And let me wash it away with the urgency of my fingertips.
Please let me talk to you in this way without any interruption…

Would you mind if we were silent for a bit?
I want these spaces to get so loud,

That you hear everything I am saying to you.
That your ears are perked to my breaths and sighs,
And your reply is simply a look we deem familiar.
An expression so subtle yet descriptive,
Where our bodies serve as the translator,
And our frequencies are tuned to the sound of our love for each other.
Please let me talk to you in this way without any interruption…

The Intensity of Fusion

Electric chemistry brews over their bodies…
Skin connecting and melting into one another,
Like warm honey into a tea, soothing their raw passion-
Cooling this heat that's been stirring for months.

A soothing calm came over the night.
Turning into a lighter tomorrow that teased their eyelids shut not long ago,
This moment was everything…
Excitement trickled from their every pore as their eyes bore into each other's souls,
Speaking "I missed you."
"I'm glad you're here."
And other utterances of words that haven't been constructed yet
But the feeling was….was…
Old and new.
Overwhelming and saddening.
Blissful and wishful of 'what if'.
So much to say that I'm speechless.

Mixed up ways I want to express this connection,
I don't know whether to sing a song,
Write a poem,
Or just hold you and let my touch speak.
But I'm weakened by your presence alone.
Strongholds on my heart strings-
I am simply in awe.
Taken aback,
Paused,
Muted,
And smiling.
All the while our energy said it all.

We danced through the sheets like ribbons of harmony-
Weaving through a masterpiece of sound.
My symphonic crescendo reverberated all over you…
When our cymbals kissed surfaces,
And your pleasurable moans echoed through my hallway,
Drizzling a storm of gratitude and appreciation.
Our breaths caught the wind-
Taking me on a ride I don't want to get off.

The care you applied to your caresses…
Undressed parts of me I wasn't sure I'd show yet,
Yet you…took your time and I could be open,
Willingly vulnerable,
And live in the Now.

The Great Orators

I imagined your water song on my petals...
Playing my favorite melody, yet new harmonies never felt so beautiful.
Finding the right key, you strike one chord and I hum final notes.

Twisted linguistics lap my overflowing cup,
Cupping your face, my wings flutter.
Shudder as you translate intent into constant, rhythmic verbiage
I'm stuttering utterances of amazement
As you shut me up in new ways...
Stating simply, "I've never met you, but you've been missed".

Kissing, sipping my words,
Quickly before my shores recede,
Listening to each wave crash,
You know exactly how to react.
Calming my seas with your storm of urgency
Swaying my swing with your winds,
Catching even slight drizzle in your bucket-
You wish to taste every drop.
Drip.
Tipping over the brim-
My honey coating your lips as I reach my dewpoint...

Words penetrating my mind,
flowing down my pleasure pathway...
Messages of intensity blooming into unspeakable bliss.
Eloquence goes out the door along with inability to articulate the pleasure I'm feeling,
Reeling and writhing more than cirque du soleil,
Needing remedial classes to form words again.
All I can do is hum sweet joy in the right key...

And my lock fits your key so well.
Swelling lower lips compelling you to receive the meal I'm providing,
Hunger like none other
…and you seem insatiable to my continuous waterfall.

Love Song(s)

With insecurities shadowed in the mask of moonlight
you undressed me.
Slowly your hands gently scanned untouched parts of my soul
Silently letting me know "I Love you Just the Way You Are"
Here the "Arms of a Woman" returned embraces and gazes upon-
this man who only knew a fraction of my attraction towards him.

I took my time exploring your favorite spots.
Fingertips skipping a blissful dance against your skin,
Writing my hearts joy and anticipation on your canvas-
In a palette of colors you unleashed in me.
We painted our feelings with wide strokes of longing and hope-
As if a taste of Heaven rested in the space between our kisses.
So sweet that I weakened at the merest brush of your lips on mine.
Trying to keep my composure yet humming "What You Do" is producing strong waves,
and all I want to do is share these "Moments in Love" with you.
Right now.

The moist droplets of my "Femininity" are quickly reaching their apex as its "Getting Late",
And I need you to feel my inner expression.
"This Feels Nice" yet "Kissing You" this deeply is piquing my imagination as to how we'd feel as one.
In this moment I can no longer allow myself to be "Without You" calming my tide...
I hate to beg but please let me wrap my "Chocolate Legs" around you tight.
Might we rock ourselves in this unsung tune while "Making Love"?
I can't take this tension anymore
Please come closer...Mmmm there you are.

Stay...
Let our "Brown Skin" melt into swirls of sweet, "Moist" love candy.
Sticking and sliding,
Winding and grinding,
Oh this "Groove With You" is like no other tempo ...
My heart beats a new "Sensuality" only for you.

If I could "Keep Getting it On" with you I would.
But I have a desire to give you another part of me.
You've opened up so much that I'm not ashamed to say
"I Want You" "In My Mouth" if that's okay...
My tongue tastes what we've written so far and I love it.
Your breath rises and falls, turning me on yet again.
"Now We're Making love" once more...
You've unlocked all doors to freedom,
So please, take all of me however you will.

"Love Won't Let Me Wait" until the next time I see you.
So, have your way and let's play until a recess is necessary.
I need not repress my emotions towards you not another minute
Hence "Nothing Even Matters" but you and I until it's time to say goodbye.
Until then, baby,
Consider our night's closeness rendering me
"Insatiable".

Flirting with Flashbacks

I want you here...
To calm this monsoon of yearning,
Urging me to use my hands,
Pretending they are yours.

I scan over parts you've kissed
Close my eyes, and breathe remembrance
Oh, the trance I was under when you sipped the words right out of me...
I became wordless but my mind said
"Don't Stop."
Don't drown in my caramel.
Be all you can be as I drip ecstasy-
And sweeten your thoughts,
Flavor the notes you play with desire and intent.

I want this night to stay with you
Play with truth and reality that we were indeed together.
Challenging distance for just this moment,
Frozen by the here and now...
And opportunity.

But I want you here,
Near the skin you caressed in the morning,
Warm bodies imploring an instant replay,
While nature envied our recreation of harmony.
Synchronicity.
Movements that drums won't dare catch,
This beat was ours alone.
An unwritten language yet to be deciphered...
All I know,
Is that I loved it.

Morning Musings

At this dawn hour, I am remembering You.
My hands graze places on my body that you've cared for so gently.
Fingertips tickling my skin's surface slowly,
I feel a surge of rising excitement while my memory-
Replays our story on the inside of my eyelids.

As I breathe in, I'm imagining your exhale above me.
Heartbeats matching our passion whilst pacing ourselves for the journey ahead.
Eyes locked in on the potential we see.
The possibilities we dare entertain beyond wishes,
And kisses that emote an eruption of this feeling.
This indescribable wave...
The explosive climax we stave off, just a little while longer.
This feels too good to rush...
So, we hush each other with each rhythmic push and pull of this dance tailored to the Love we share.

At this dawn hour, I recall...
Your tender knocking at my entrance.
My welcoming to your thoughtful offer to give yourself to me-
Trusting that I'd hold your heart,
Hold you,
Hold that most intimate piece of you,
With the same peace and admiration that I notice when you gaze upon me.
I wanted you to feel the warm, moist security envelop this gift wrapped in chocolate-
As you meet this brown sugar glaze all over you...
I wanted my nectar to sweeten those pieces of you that got soured to the thought that you're not a priority.

Because all I see…is You.
And this truth can't be hidden behind "too soon",
"Hold up" or "wait".
Our fate seems to be written by a force beyond us-
Pushing us to a familiarity that feels foreign yet like home in the same breath.

So, at this hour, I'm remembering our chemistry…
This unsaid thing that takes me over,
Surrounds me with warmth and assurance.
The purity of your presence that allows me to Breathe
Experience
Enjoy
And just be.

I smile even at thoughts that brought me here.
Fear has no place in this forward movement,
A major improvement to what I'm used to.
Being used by fools who assumed I'd be ride or die,
But dying inside is no trophy-
In fact, it's a scarlet letter I'd regret walking around with.

But with you laying next to me in this bed,
In this life,
A pure light shines over and around us.
Insulating our passion and sealing in this vision,
Like the hidden puzzle piece that completes the picture,
Your affection is the glue that holds my days together.
Treasuring my memories
And sitting in anticipation of the next time we can awaken wrapped in last night's secrets,
And do this all over again…

Book 6: I am Evolving.

Opaque Reflections of Clarity

People say that darkness is bad…
Yet in the stillness of the morning,
Before the sun wakes up,
The world is so peaceful.

The ensemble of silence creates a symphony.
Playing the right chords to my soul.
A classical masterpiece-
Composed of dreams I'm trying to remember,
And don't want to let go of.

My heartbeat keeps rhythm with my inner awakening thoughts,
And is always the right pace…
My breathing is even as I ask God what He wants me to learn,
To accomplish today.

And there's actually space to listen.
So many conversations happen in silence…
We just have to be tuned in,
To hear what they are saying.

Inverse Reality

One day I saw the moon at noon while the sun was shining.
A reminder that beginnings and endings are fluid and not static-
That this room is just for practice,
Preparing us for the next level of eternity and purpose.

The sunrises and sunsets are so similar in beauty.
That our duty is to work within this dichotomy,
And do our best,
Knowing each side has a motivation.

Darkness has a meaning…
And that confusion is normal when viewing two opposing energies in the same space.
But, this is life.
A warped knot of existence where all feelings are welcome.
Various potential outcomes,
Full of 'What If's and 'I wonder'…
When the sun slumbers does it continue to shine?
When the moon rests, does it wish it had more time?
To be mere morsel of what the sun can do…
Or do both, strong in their own right
And Just Be.

The wisdom of acceptance and embrace
Two entities of the same spectrum occupying their lane
And being okay with it.

I saw the moon at noon while the sun was shining.
A reminder that beginnings and endings are fluid and not static…

The Price of Competence

To be strong doesn't mean you go looking for a fight

To be strong means you're wishing with all your might-

That today may be a day you can put your armor down and just be

That today may be a day you can rest free-

Of impending battles,

Inevitable struggles,

Never ending troubles that challenge your will.

Those strides uphill that throb with every step

Those stabs to the core when you've got nothing left but you're strong, right

You can handle it right?

This plight is light work to those who've been born to fight

Not quite.

Atmospheric Shifts

Whirlwinds swirling new life events around me…

Inhaling deeply to catch this new breath refreshing my outlook,

That I too, can have the desires of my heart.

Seasons of cold results,

Scolding my naïveté that they were the one,

Evolved into reasons the puzzle pieces were jagged-

Ragged and frayed edges of broken souls.

Rubbing two quarters of remains trying to make a whole,

And I was good for being the fixer.

Mixing scraps together trying to make a meal that would last a lifetime.

Yet God saved me and sat me down.

Grounded me to examine the foundation that was always a little muddy,

Always a little soft, allowing rotten soil to seep in-

But deep in my heart

I believe this "new" is right on time.

The clocks paused,

Stalled long enough to see the missteps.

The strides on cracks I thought were solid,

But all I did this last time was reflect…

Wait…

And here I am.

Homage to Stevie

I am moved by the twang of his delivery;
The intricacies his ribbon weaves through chords and melodies.
The precision of his choices
Handpicked notes dropped into symphonies,
Delighting my ears with sweet dripping morsels of genius
He was a prodigy.
A Wonder.

Boggling our understanding of normalcy,
He effortlessly mastered crafts while we were in our infancy of what music was.
His rifts render goosebumps,
Prickling my skin with a newfound love of musical vulnerability.
An ear always in tune with what I never had the courage to say
He wrote it like stolen pages of my secrets,
Skeletons in my closet,
My bones breaking to break beats,
Syncopation making me pause in awe of everything that is Stevie.

Anything I felt, he said it
Seeds of longing I planted, he bred it-
Into flowers of joy I wore in my headphones.
Begging he never leave my side,
My strides in life mirror "Songs in the Key of Life"
And he has A Major part of why lyrics move my own work.
I will be forever inspired by a man who sees songs-
While being blinded physically.
He paints experience on a canvas,
Scribed by his interpretation of what love is.
How beautiful his presence moves me,
Grooves me into forgetting my troubles
For as long as the song lasts...

Familial Patterns

These patterns I try to shatter come from a lineage of dysfunction.
Punctuated by excuses and confusion,
Leading to passive aggression.
My confession is...I am the same
My difference is I am aware of it.

I watch my shortcomings come alive in the blind,
Missteps on cracks breaking more than backs for ages.
The shade is cool, but I like it in the sun-
Where the rays unearth my insecurities,
Fear becomes undone.
Revealing truth...and flaws,
Unmasked so I can work on them,
Openly and willingly vulnerable.

These patterns are like argyle and plaid.
Tangled branches from the sum of my trees,
Fighting to weed off what doesn't work for me,
While attempting not to scorch the earth that secures my walk.
Resulting in hypervigilance,
Afraid of quaking on faults I wasn't alive to create.
Such an intricate tango...
Tip-toeing around repeated mistakes while tapping to others'
unrealistic expectations.
Hesitations to be my own unique standard,
With hands stirring old ways of thinking,
Sprinkled with wisdom and mishaps.

I feel trapped between individuality and conformity.
I get zapped by foreshadowing prophesies that told me I should
know better.
Recoiling, I lick my wounds.

Bandaging up sores so deep I can't keep away the recurring infections to our ancestry.
There isn't enough tapestry to smother the flames.
I blame no one, though.
Each cohort sorted out their messes and did their best with what they had.
Survival of the most skilled at resilience-
Resisting the urge to succumb to the typical excuses.

I take that strength and strap it to my knapsack.
Like a feather in my hat,
I marvel at the duality of where we were
And how far we've come.
I hum a tune of perseverance.
A familiar melody reminiscent of a Motherland tempo,
Married with the Western ego that I can have it all.
I do a call and response to everyone whose chorus elevated me to this place of acceptance,
And with this chance to excel above and beyond,
I take the challenge.

Pursuing Foreverland

Why am I chasing something most are trying to escape?
Something people don't appreciate once they have it…
Love-attracting habits turn into the ghost of Christmas past.
This institution where you feel trapped,
But you willingly vowed to commit,
Until it all falls down.
The moments that call for extreme patience,
Persistence,
A remembrance of the reasons you're there in the first place,
Yet everyone says it changes with that proclamation,
"I now pronounce you"
You devoted your life to…?
Argue. Deceive. Omit.
Leave the real you hidden until,
The dead bolt has sealed your destiny *then* it gets serious?
Was the carrot dangled,
Then mangled in the blender along with who you used to be?
A lost identity
And this is what I want…

The green I glean regarding my freedom.
The facility I have that no one depends on me.
No suspending my goals or dreams for anyone,
Rendering boundless aspirations where only I stand in my way
Yet…this is the marathon I train for.
When many are dying to run away, I take practice trips
Jogs around a field of maybe,
Stealing looks at the finish line,
Of what exactly?

Pressure-filled Intentions

The way it's supposed to be is a dash of fantasy,
With many pieces of reality
Mixed in with sh** happens-
And we will get through it together.
God's got it.
God's got us.

The way it's supposed to be is mostly-met expectations
Coupled with learned acceptance-
That you realize the hype is just that.
But forget that,
Because what you have is real.
What you have, you feel deep in your bones-
Beyond anything you've imagined.

'Supposed to be' is a set up.
A jumbled bowl of should and 'musturbations'
Full of one-sided misconceptions leading down a path of-
'Why did I ever think that?'

'Supposed to be' are the magazines that flash the glitter.
But never show the sweat and tears poured into-
Keeping the seams of a union together.
Threads screaming for anything but mending…
Unraveling ideals with each disagreement,
As two try to find one language,
Their vernacular unique to their chemistry.
Yet, all of this is underneath blankets of multigenerational curses.

The first plan of action necessary
Is to throw away 'supposed to be'.
Embrace what is.

And determine if this yields a possibility of hers and his.
Monogrammed towels,
Self-written vowels,
Gazebos of churches filled with lovers of love,
Looking upon passionate gazes as they blaze a path
Others know will be bumpy.

Crumpled up favors stepped on by naysayers-
Who only came to judge the bouquets.
The ones they wish they caught…
Oh, but 'supposed to be' seeks out the ones-
Swept away by fairytales and tradition.
Suckers leeching onto trending surprise proposals,
Painting their perfect picture so that whomever-
Will just have to get with the program.
Insert robot here
The issue is we fear the possibility of difference feeling right.
Unconventional shining bright,
And overpowering boxes and rules.
So much commentary on how to get married-
With little attention of how to **be** married.

Commercialism and unspoken competition have aptly shielded us-
From being enlightened in the freedom of truth.
And that is… 'Supposed to be' is antiquated.
Frozen in eras where UHF and VHF were our only choices.
Where the only voices we minded came from our parents,
And grandparents whose lines were defined by the times in which they dwelled.
Yet the bell has rang long ago to wake up-
And consider scripting your own story.
Make 'supposed to be' an agreement between you two alone.
A strong bond so custom-made that you feel nothing but
Unmistakably free.

Plight of a Healer

With tears streaming down her face
She told me "I don't deserve to be happy."
The words hit me in my gut.
The cut of her pain bled my soul in deep compassion.
The fact that she rationed joy into portions-
For everyone but herself.
Needs on a shelf and scraping the plate for leftovers,
What a hell this is.

Speechless is a rarity…
For I was muted by this disparity,
That something so priceless was outside of her reach!
My heart cried for her.
My internal tears made my vision unclear of where to go next.
So, I inhaled her pain,
And exhaled a silent prayer of wisdom.
A begging for a restoration of anything I'd learned,
I yearned for words to come out and said
"You do deserve to be happy."

My challenge sat in the boxing ring-
Ding, Ding.
Round 1 goes to us both unmasking ourselves-
Gloves off,
And digging in.
The only thing I could rely on was our alliance.
A compliance to an unspoken contract-
That I'd never give up on her…
Never live with accepting unhappiness as an option.

In that moment, I understood a glacier dwelled under her iceberg,
And she was frozen by what she endured.

With our paths slowly coming to a sunset,
We promised to work as hard as we could in the daylight.
Chipping away with all of our power,
Until her troubles began to surrender their grip
On her happiness.

Simple Rules

The rules are simple: secure your mask before helping others.
How often we forget to save ourselves.
Put our needs on the forefront,
So we can become whole and not cut pieces of our core we-
In actuality, don't have to offer.

We deplete our tanks into fumes,
And assume we have full capacity to operate.
Our fate lies in the quality of self-care,
For there's where we need to be at our best.
Feeding our minds, bodies, souls
In order to impart highest quality in everything we touch…
See…
Influence…
If we're not congruent to what we speak-
What good are we?

Who Heals the Healer

We help singed souls

We walk with tired cries

We guide the lost with our own blinders on

Hoping our shades don't dim their light

We empathize with their plight while fighting our own

Therefore, we juggle multiple struggles,

Praying we don't drop a tidbit of others pain.

We get caught in the rain soaked with daily sorrow,

Setbacks and disappointments...

Yet we rarely make appointments to sit with our own stuff.

It gets stuffed in the bag along with schedules,

Timelines,

And missed opportunities to breathe...

Reflect...

Put it down.

Let God take it all while He hands out a more reasonable plate.

We hate to ask for help because we *are* the help

qui est Medicus sanat, we ask

Who heals the healer?

Will You Be There?

I'd like to invite you to my last days…
No, no – see I don't plan on going anywhere soon,
I'm just saying that right now,
If this is the last moment we speak,
I want you to be able to say something good.
Don't say what we could have done.
The missed opportunities to connect,
The times we wrecked the present,
On some looking back or looking forward ish

But I'm saying, right now,
If this is the last time we speak,
Would you come?
Would you celebrate the laughs, the insight
The ideas we ignited in the air,
Without a care for the future?
Would you celebrate the time, time stood still
So we could dwell a little longer,
Breathe the same air,
Building stronger ties between our hearts,
Tying knots that not even distance could unravel.

See, I want you to know…I'm here.
I think about you more than I mention.
My attention is on the must-do's,
The need-to's,
And the I didn't do's,
I rinse and repeat feeling defeated at the amount of adulting-
I didn't accomplish.
But this…
You…are important to me.
I want to deposit so much good into us

That there is no doubt, you'd be there.
No hesitation that we constructed something special that you want to share,
There…

With everyone listening…
Relating to those precious moments,
The inside jokes.
The plans we hoped would manifest.
I need you to know that I wanted the best for our connection,
Nothing less.
That our time was indeed frozen,
And only thawed by responsibility.
Melting into cracks I thought were as sealed,
As the concrete I built these dreams on.

That being said, may we take advantage of 'here'?
Each year that flies by
I think of the wings we painted in the canvases of our minds.
The boundless aspirations we bounced off each other.
The cover we found in the blankets of understanding,
That only occurs with time, attention and patience
So, I'm asking…
Before 'there' happens
Can I see you 'here'?
I'll be waiting…

Glowing Innocence

She was golden...
Holding a life that shone through her and around her,
Hope beaming from her womb.
She gave everyone promise.
Broken spirits suddenly seeking repair in order to prepare their influence on the new being.
He changed everyone before he emerged.
Unchained melodies of multigenerational flaws-
All came down to this moment of truth.

The knowledge of his upcoming arrival bud a hidden excitement to be better,
To be stronger,
To belong more to a maturity that he'd see and want to mimic.
Oh, how the droves of people unearthed their shortcomings to renew the ties that bind.
No more hiding betwixt trees rooted in poisonous foundations.
No more retractions of hurt feelings sweeping them under the rug.

He made everyone expose the unfinished wood.
He moved them to sandpaper the roughness until it was as smooth as his unborn skin.
The bumps were more visible...
More visceral,
Easier to tackle but more painful to bring out the tools packed long ago.
Tools worn down from mishandling the delicacy of unconditional love,
Tattered and torn from mix-matching purpose and pride.

They strived to be a prize he'd keep his eyes on.
A redesigned drive with detours explaining what not to do-

While waving from the roads they paved with unwise decisions.

She was golden,
And he was a child so grand.
Just the idea of his entrance made everyone stand at attention.
Saluting and bowing at the humble chance to get it right,
Be better,
And do better,
For him.

Book 7: I am Resilient.

Eagerly Anticipating…

I am looking forward to something to look forward to.
Searching for the next door-
That leads to more than dead ends.
Mending these stitches in time,
Trying to patch together the holes that-
Life has dealt me.

I am looking forward to smiling…
Not just at past memories.
Not the fake, teeth-showing,
Lifeless eyes knowing the truth,
But a full, bright grin that reflects-
The color of my soul.

I am looking forward to comfort within this space,
Through this storm,
For the clouds to break apart.
And show my heart the reasons-
For this season.
For night to fall,
Where I don't call out for solace.

I am looking forward to peace.

Fleeting Recollections

I used to know this girl...
Big eyes, bigger heart,
Flawless start.
Wore a long white dress to the playground-
'Cause she never got dirty.
Played it safe...
Watched all the other kids dive first
Get hurt,
But not her...

Smoothing out her lace and ruffles,
Trouble unknown to her perfect bubble.
Watched from afar of how good, bad looked
But never partook,
Content with a book and hope.
She asked me if I would hold her hand,
While she took in this new land.
The area was uncharted-
And she didn't want to start off wrong.

I agreed...
Letting her know things would speed up at times,
Like the merry go round she loved so much,
Minus the levers she couldn't help but touch.
This ride would be different.
Years passed on,
Dress not so long,
Had to cut the sleeves so her body could breathe in-
New experience.

Now she's partially exposed...
Soap can't wash off everything so the dress had a new shade-

Call it dingy reality.
Actually got used to the sweat stains of pained truth.
Life's proof that no one is invincible,
Nor untouchable.
Yes lovable, but ever permeable to-
The up's and down of growing up.
I couldn't protect her like I wanted to,
And it was heart-breaking.
She kept making calls out to me,
Screaming for help.
Somewhere along the line I put her needs on a shelf,
Considered everyone else's,
Concerned with what they thought,
What they sought,
Wasn't hard to tell…

I fought myself daily in a present-day hell over who to put first.
Overwhelmed by the undying thirst for answers,
Her voice cracked, crying for recognition.
The position I put her in was unforgivable,
Damn near unlivable,
Yet she kept her trust in me…
Regardless of my worthiness to-
Be the protector of something so dear.

Some days, she would just look at me-
Wiping away tears,
Failing at hiding the fear she encountered along the way.
The little girl was still in there…
Somewhere…
Though, something was missing.
Her hair had a stench of liquor and lust
Substitutes for what her real path should have been-

Her heart covered in rust
And she just looked at me...

Those big eyes told a story of disappointment.
Missed appointments of where the blessings were assigned.
Told me rash decisions took her place in line.
Every time they took a piece of her-
She was willing to give it.
Living off the hope of receiving the same,
But that day never came.

Unreciprocated efforts whittled her sweetness away-
To nothingness.
Always loving less than she deserved.
Her people pleasing tendencies had her teasing her own emotions-
unfulfilled.
Naïve to sleazy intentions,
And her only prevention was to be alone.
But that's not what her heart called home...

She brought the dress back to me lying in a box.
Said the only way to avoid further damage-
Was to keep it sealed and locked.
She didn't want to lose it but leaving it out for everyone-
Was a magnet for abuse.
I asked her what she wore...
She said she just tightens the belt around a black robe
When she answers the door,
Don't get dressed no more,
She knew what they were there for.

And I just looked at her...
And it.
The pure white frock had turned to a shade of brown

Like the kids from the park stomped it to the ground
The lace was gone; ruffles lost their fluff.
The delicate trim was wrinkled,
This dress had had enough.

At this point it was unwearable
Irreparable
The biggest patches known to man couldn't cover up the holes- Left by them stroking,
Poking in their needs and leaving her seeds to rot-
Rarely nurtured by true love's moist soil.

Relying on the rain to be her only spoil
While toiling to hold onto whatever's left in her,
What's **left** in her?
A future where perhaps things would look up?
What luck she would have to run into to build up her defeated trust

And she just…looked at me.
Her hair was wet from the constant troubles-
Showering down on head.
She cowered in the corner of the tub instead of-
Standing up and dealing with it.

Finally, she rose to her feet.
Stopped bobbing to the beats of the wrong drums-
She'd rather listen to herself hum.
The misguiding music was blaring so loud -
That I could never hear her.
I used my towel to wipe the fog off the mirror,
Looked her deep into those big brown eyes,
And told her, "I can't promise you anything but-
I'll do my best to protect you better this time…"

I Needed You

If you've felt my absence
Lacking our time spent
I'm short with replies
Even more sparse with time
It's not that you did something....
It's that some things did me in.
Spinning me to the dark side of life
Strife.
Quite hard to deal with a waterfall of trouble
When a paper cup holds your last bit of luck,
Subtlety breaking a fragile bubble-
And once it's broken...
Like two snowflakes
You can never duplicate what you wish would stay the same.

Don't blame yourself
Can't have shame on what was dealt
But I've been dealing
Wheeling on two broken axles-
With no Escape button in sight.
Can't even Control the Alternatives
So I must Delete and Start over.
My point is....
Instead of noting the void of "Me"
Stop avoiding me
Taking it personally
That my Ring ID doesn't show up as frequently.
The depression suppressing me might your cue
A clue that in this hour, I needed you.

Like smelling salts after a knockout.
When I'm lost out to sea, be my Lighthouse.

Guide me back with your bright light
Make me feel right once again
I needed you to be that empty chamber
During a game of Roulette
Saving me from myself, not letting me forget
There's Something to live for…

I needed you to hold the steering wheel
When I wanted to let go
Veering me back to color within the lines-
I know like the back of my hand.
The land got a little rocky so I needed you to be my tread.
Help me strengthen my grip on the Rough side of the mountain
Lengthen my strides, Not to the fountain of youth
I'd rather the fountain of truth-
So I can swallow easier why things have to be this way.

Maybe you couldn't handle my valleys…
You were so used to my peaks,
I kept you so high
Perhaps we couldn't survive at ground zero.
And I've grown up a bit so the bottle can't be my hero.
Changed my stride from sneaks to stilettos-
And had to let go of some bad habits.

I needed your full attention.
The tension playing in my head was nearing explosion
Erosion of my most pure hopes and dreams
Weaned itself off the breast of innocence,
Leaving me bare,
Starving for one morsel of restoration.
Elation that maybe, just maybe this is all one f***ed up mind trip.

And I'll never be able to slip that info into a text message,
Or between songs,
So, I wish you'd have come along-
And kept me company on my Road to recovery.
The slap in the face was the discovery that maybe
You were only solar-powered
But even the sun goes down and endures its dark hours
So, during that time
I…
Needed…
You already know the rest.

Where I thought there was a nest,
An empty branch stood.
Like a bird, you migrated to warm weather.
I wish I could.
But I was right here,
The whole time.
Climbing slowly but surely.
Right here.
Restoring my faith,
Right here.
And I'm *still*
Right here!
Not waiting, but relating to the people-
Old and new that held me up and brought me through-
No matter what and remained
Right here.

A Half-Full/Half-Empty Greeting

How are you?
I'm fine. And you?
I'm good.
Who cares?
Not you.
One word can't define how I'm doing,
So, I'll describe 'til I ruin your expectations of a short reply.

I'm anxious.
Anxious to know what it's gonna be
Who it's gonna be
And am I gonna be happy with that
And when is *that* gonna be?

I'm frustrated
Frustrated with "if"
Dying to move to the land of "is" and "is not"
Seems to be light years away, these days.
My rocket's losing gas
Gushing out fast
Need to patch that up
Before I crash
Land on "Maybe".

I'm afraid.
Afraid of losing half of me
23 chromosomes that gave me these eyes
This tenacity
The sweetheart in me.
Struggling constantly with inevitability.
She holds my sanity,
And when she can't

Who got me?

I'm sure you must go by now
Thought I'd fake it again somehow but I'm tired…
Tired of plastering this smile,
This veneer is losing its luster.
Can't muster up enough sheen to slip to a better state of mind
But yeah I'm fine.
And you?
I'm good.
Who cares?
Not you.

"Can" took a vacation
Subletted to "Can't"
Therefore I can't brush it off, the bristles are worn
Can't snap out of it, my fingers are torn-
On hope's jagged edge.
See this is where I live right now,
Looking over the hedge.
Wondering if it's true-
That over there's a brighter hue.

I'm slipping.
Slipping on the buttons of life's Etch-O-Sketch.
Straight lines are supposed to be easy…right?
Not without light.
Wait…
Almost got it
F***.
Hit another bump
Shook my whole sh** up.

So here I am at the line once again,

Ready to dash out the blocks.
Sneaks got stolen; I'm workin' with socks.
Holes in those.
Squinting to see my lane
It's starting to rain
This could get tricky
Like Bambi's try at ice… wasn't pretty.

But I'm trying.
Trying to find my niche in a life with occupied corners.
The middle of the floor isn't fun without someone to dance with.
To Love.
Laugh.
Live.
LIFE.

So, I'm living.
Never giving up
Just gets tough to brave the cold,
When I just told myself to shed some layers-
Let the sun touch my Soul.
I need relief
If relief were fresh air, my window would be painted open Forever.
No matter the weather.
Things must get better.
They always do
Patience is a virtue
Never been more true.

You picked the wrong one today
Weren't prepared for what I had to say
And I'm fresh outta sugar
Got too heavy,
Price became too hefty.

Now, "F*** it!" was on sale
Displayed right next to TMI
So I apologize if I'm wasting your time.
Took the other pill for a change
So I wasn't able to comply with the required script.
I know you ain't diggin' this dose of the real me...
Lemme slip on the cloak again, make it easy .
Go 'head.
Repeat.
I'm ready...

How are you?
Oh I'm fine. And you?
I'm good.
Who cares?
Not you.

Cocoon

In this cocoon I have wrapped around myself-
I am safe and peaceful.
No loud outbursts permeating my being,
I am simply Being.

Enjoying the silent pleasure of my breath
Resting, stretching to my furthest horizons
Arriving at realizations once ignored
No mystery doors 1, 2 and 3 revealing misery.
No surprise daggers to my heart,
For there is a soft shell there
Just hard enough to shield from harm-
But flexible enough allow tenderness.

Rendering me to new experiences that are much welcomed.
Rebirthing my existence and seeing how wide my wings can spread,
When not held down by stifling boxes,
Where even deep breathing is frightening.
Treading this path ever so carefully to avoid repeated storms where my wings could get wet.
Weighing me down when I was born to fly,
Born to flutter around untraveled places and find my own way
God made mental brakes for us
So U-turns are okay…

In this space it's all allowed within reason.
And I'm thankful to dance in an empty room,
Not lonely, just only me and my thoughts.
Letting internal tunes sway me as I lean and rock-
To the steps He has ordered for me.
This…feels….right
As bright as the returned twinkle in my eyes,

Resembling the stars I've always reached for and will continue to.

This cocoon is warm...
Heating up the icy portions frozen over to protect,
I am finally letting myself thaw.
Glisten in the sun while the pain melts off of me-
And seeps into the gutters where it belongs,
Along with shortened songs of broken promises
clipped wings
and pieces of me left unnurtured.

In this cocoon I can sing as loudly as I please!
Glee resounding inside these walls I have painted yellow.
Resembling the weather of my being.
Clever, intricate notes bellowing to their full potential,
Weaving in and out of beautiful melodies seamlessly
As tightly knit as renewed trust and joy.
Quilting new stitches in time and space,
Continuing to learn me again.
To forgive an old friend I left in caring for others
It's time for me and She to connect and become One.
One way to be me instead of contorting faces,
Makeup changes to fit their concept of what looks good
I'm just fine!

Just redefining lines left up to question, judge and deem unconventional
Barefaced leaves me pure and able to see what I've been hiding from.
Exfoliating mistakes and writing my future once again,
Until I say it's right.
Until I say it's right.
Until I say it's right!
I do not need advice on what you did when

And how you handled…
And what you think I…
I got this.

Dieu M'Envoie des Fleurs

He told me "God sends me flowers and you are one of them"
I didn't know if that made me a gardenia, hydrangea or a hyacinth
But I knew I only wanted to be a help…
A joy in tumultuous period with an unknown end.
I wanted to live up to the beauty a flower possesses,
Delicate to the touch,
Standing strong in the sun and even the rain.

I wanted to be tender and sway with wherever the wind took us.
I prayed for the shady days to not overshadow my brightness.
For no slights in the weather to alter our climate of peace.
I gave encouragement likened to the faith of a mustard seed.
Breeding disbelief that my small frame could shoulder the boulders of unexpected tomorrows.
Even sorrow couldn't shake my rooting in God that it'd be alright,
That he'd be alright.

I stood strong in the unforced fields of discovery.
We frolicked in possibility knowing only He had the final answer.
Beyond mishaps and shortcomings of man,
Despite the fear that sunrise would arrive without him.
He held strong to his flower…
Powerful hands never loosened their grip on hope and the power of prayer.
Layers of doubt washed off with each morning his eyes met another day…
And another day…

I'd prune off weeds of sadness before I'd attempt to be what he saw in me.
Making sure my petals were in full bloom.
No tears when Heaven is much better than here.

No uncertainty when he had such surety in salvation.
As I look back, I can only hope I was even a fraction of the joy and beauty flowers convey.
But just in case I was not
On his last birthday, I sent a bouquet…

Dreams Deferred by the Clock

Time, I need to talk to you…
If you'd please grant me your wares,
I know they are priceless-
Yet if you could offer me credit
I'd take anything you offer for more moments with him.

Time, how frugal you were with us
I thought we had more pieces of you banked-
Into our accounts of dreams and future goals.
We were so sure we budgeted enough to insure us for a lifetime,
But you had a different plan.
Rendering us bankrupt before we played our full game.

Oh, Time how cruel you can be
I know we borrowed, robbed and try to cheat our way to get more of you
But it was all for Love.
So, it was fair. Right?
For love, we put in all our chips,
Rested on faith,
Leaned on the Lord
Prayed for more of you to enter our lives,
To bless us with the manifestation of aspirations discussed,
To create a blending of the best parts of us.
More boundless bliss.
But our fingertips lost our grip on you.
We tried everything to hold onto you,
And you, Time, you fled us in the night.
Blind-sighted by your trickery,
I was knocked senseless into the reality
That you were indeed not on my side.

Time…you fickle spinster of joy and pain,
What more could I have done?
I was loyal to you and cherished you to the fullest.
I packed much purpose into the gift you gave me with him,
And you played with me.
Dangled the carrot and I bit down so hard and fast
That we were speechless with happiness.

Now, Time, I know I gripped you by the reins,
And begged you to grant me things you could not.
For you knew the answers and held them close to your heart.
So, I know I'm asking for an oasis in the desert of my mind-
That yearns for his love to keep refreshing me,
But please humor my irrational plea and wish that I had more of you…
For Us.

As I Escape to Slumber

Meet me in my dreams, Love…
Let us join hands as always,
And walk in your Heaven.
Show me around your life's work
To the place you graduated
Where you reaped the rewards you so longed for,
And we're all trying to get to.
Let us escape into a realm where reality is a cloud, far far away
All I want is **us.**
In a still moment where our seamless harmony made butterflies dance.
Where our whispers spoke volumes to each other's desires.
I miss…this.

Meet me in my dreams, Love…
Allow our reunion to comfort my soul.
For my heart to be whole yet again even if it's mere mindplay
I need a brief fallacy to soothe my dark nights
For you knighted me with the gift of holding your heart,
And I did so, willingly and without complaint.
Life was light and so were my steps through our path.
And now as I walk alone-
I yearn for your warmth by my side.

Meet me in my dreams, Love…
I need your hand once more to stroke my hair,
Comb over my brokenness,
Smooth my edges of sadness,
Remove the strands of doubt that I'll never be cherished like this again.
Help me see clearly through this cold season,
And continue to look upward and onward as you did.

Your touch healed mountains of mishaps.
Your words calmed seas of unease
With minimal yet powerful words:
"I'm here."
And you still are…
I hear you tell me to breathe when I'm stressed.
I hear you say "ignore foolishness" during nonsensical unrest.
I see your joy when snowflakes hit the ground.
I feel you swaying me with your favorite gospel sounds.
You are here!
I know this.
Yet my tears fall into a boundless pool of unfulfilled destiny
Streams of my sorrow track the face you deemed-
"beautiful with HD eyes".

So, realize I catch myself looking for you, Love…
My slumber throws a nightly plea
A begging that we can meet, repeat and add on-
To a story written so beautifully and effortlessly.
But sometimes a pen loses ink,
Leaving one to think "how could it have ended".
However, I cherish our commas and spaces no one sees between our parentheses,
And for those I thank you, Love.
Thus, for this night, and many
Please steal me away.
Refresh me with your presence that made my heart beam-
And meet me in my dreams.

Letter to My Angel

I hope you're proud of me…
I just want to do well in your eyes.
I realize you've springboarded me to greatness,
A confidence within that was undiscovered.
You uncovered my best,
Challenged me to "do my thing fully"
And fearlessly.

I'm questioning my next chapters…
Remembering you always told me to go after whatever I wanted,
And with that I'm taking steps into the unknown.
I've grown to understand nothing is impossible-
Except the barriers we create.
Our mind manifests doubts negating our dreams,
And we conveniently get comfortable with the status quo.
But you, you willed me to go for it.
Whatever it was, you supported me.
For with that foundation of boundless love
And unconditional intentions
I stand tall.

About the Author

La'Shawn Janell: A wearer of many hats but those closest to her heart are parenting, counseling and having authentic interactions with others. Therapist, college instructor, model, basketball player and closet DJ are other titles that follow this lover of words.

La'Shawn started writing at the age of 14 but did not perform her first piece until age 20 at her alma mater, University of Delaware at an open mic event for an organization called S.P.I.T. (Stimulating Prose, Ideas and Theories). 2007 opened a new world of possibilities and she was encouraged to perform her pieces more consistently in Philadelphia, PA at the Arts Garage, Warmdaddy's, A Poet's Art Gallery and many other local venues in Delaware and New Jersey as well. She had the privilege of being one of the opening poets for Celia, of French musical duo "Les Nubians". La'Shawn was also selected as a feature poet for television show "Conscious Poetry".

Along with performing these personal pieces, La'Shawn was part of the Open Words poet collective and assisted with co-hosting and holding monthly open mic events in PA and NJ. Her writings tend to be personal but encompass a relatability that all can connect to. Throughout her works contain universal life themes that often boil down to our undeniable search for Love, Freedom and Belonging.

About the Title

The more I grow, the more I am shaped by the difference between what I thought and what I have learned. Butterflies are ever-changing, especially in the beginning. As we ingest experiences and process them, the only thing that is consistent, is change. I've always seen myself as a butterfly; one that needs to soar and be free in order to feel whole. So, 'Evolution of a Butterfly's Truth' defines a collection of realities I have learned through trial and error, risk and reward, and everything in between. The walk through emotional and physical freedom continues to influence my journey; and I've only just begun.

Acknowledgments

My parents: I have several parental figures (my village is quite powerful) but I have always said that you two, Mom and Dad have created a beautiful monster 😊 My quick wit, my way with words, my love of love coupled with my ferocious tenacity and passion for all things fair and just, clearly comes from you both! Thank you for supporting my verbal development and artistic nature, allowing me to ascend while having a firm grip on reality. With your love and encouragement, I stand courageous and brave, seeking truth and settling for *no less* than greatness.

My son, CJD: Your Light brightens my world. Your smile and laugh remind me to always find happiness in what I do and pursue, and that joy cannot be taken by anyone. You are my mirror, reflecting my good, bad and ugly and you call me on it with a wisdom and insight that is well beyond your young years. You, Son, are the reason I make my choices and strive to be the best Mother I can be. Your eyes search my soul, daring me to remain honest on this path. I thank God for you daily.

My Love: That moment when you know you're going to know someone forever, no matter what 😊 Your encouragement, love and listening has been like drinking my favorite coffee while listening to our self-named playlist: Warm. Comforting. Right on Time. The safety and security I feel by your presence is rare yet familiar and I thank you for walking along with me through this. It is with that support that I've been able to be comfortable with the uncomfortable, take risks and trust that all will work out. Thank you for giving me room to spread my wings, achieve one of my dreams and share it with you.

Vilas Pagan-Afanador: I did it. You planted the seed more than 5 years ago and finally I have risen to the challenge! Thank you for being one of my biggest fans and encouragers of my work. The mark you left on this world and many people's hearts still has ripple effects and your impact is immeasurable. The rest you already know, and I have felt your loving presence throughout this process, like the angel that you are, whispering over my shoulder to "do your thing". Keep flying high and watching over us, Superman.

My publisher Dave Ware Jr.: You saw me perform 5 years back and also planted the thought that bloomed into this tree of creation with bountiful branches of my story. Thank you for believing in my gift!

My fellow Poets/Artists: Y'all are something else. You wordsmiths, benders of language, professors of prose, and ninjas of nouns, verbs, participles and transitions. I am repeatedly humbled when I come around you. The ways your brains work is mind-boggling, and I pause when I think about how you see *me* as a part of your community. Your feedback has been uplifting, reassuring and validating that I needed to share this gift. The gratitude I have regarding your faith in my words and delivery is enough to shed a tear. Thank you *so* much for the features, spotlights, hosting opportunities, shout-outs and mentions. Every time I hit a stage, it feels like Home and many times like Church. I appreciate all of your positive energy lighting this path of discovery. Much Love.

Friends and family: There aren't enough pages or lines to describe the warmth I feel when thinking about how you all have lifted me up through the years. The triumphs and challenges you have witnessed have been interesting to watch I'm sure, however it is with your love and wisdom that I keep walking, striving and achieving. Thank you 1 million times over for the conversations, vent sessions, open ears, welcoming homes and rewarding interactions. I definitely could not live this life alone; I appreciate you for walking with me on this journey of evolution. I soar…simply because you told me I could.

WARERESOURCES AND PUBLISHING
WE ARE AN ALL IN ONE,
ONE STOP PUBLISHING COMPANY!!!!

W.R.P. is a modest but skillful and knowledgeable Christian Publishing Company. We specialize in getting authors into print. We embrace and guide each author like a member of our family. We treat you fairly and recognize the importance of building a lasting relationship with you as an author. Join us in the walk to promote prosperity along with the message of encouragement and peace. Be one of the authors we transform and prepare for the world of information and books.

FEEL FREE TO CONTACT US@

www.wareresources.com

1-800-469-4850 EXT. 2

http://www.facebook.com/pages/Ware-Resources-and-Publishing

www.ingramcontent.com/pod-product-compliance
Lightning Source LLC
Chambersburg PA
CBHW050554300426
44112CB00013B/1919